Discover
English

Language analysis for teachers

Rod Bolitho
Brian Tomlinson

MACMILLAN

Macmillan Education
Between Towns Road, Oxford OX4 3PP
A division of Macmillan Publishers Limited
Companies and representatives throughout the world

ISBN 1-4050-8003-5

First published 1980, New edition 1995, This edition 2005

Designed by Mike Brain
Illustrated by Maggie Ling

The publishers and authors would like to thank the following for
permission to reproduce material in this book:

Pelican Books for *How Children Fail* by John Holt.
Observer Magazine for *Delicious Discoveries No. 1: Beenleigh Blue Cheese* by Drew Smith.
Longman for *English for Electrical Engineers* by J. McAllister and G. Madanna.
The Independant for *Patten says tests will go ahead.*
The Guardian for *Dial M for Murder by Mother.*

Cover photo by © apply pictures/Alamy

Printed in Thailand

2008 2007 2006 2005
8 7   6 5   4 3   2 1

Contents

Introduction

What sort of English should we teach?

66 I want my students to speak only the best English, so I encourage them to read only the classics of English literature."

Is this a good idea?

How much do we really know about English?

True or false?

* *Some* is only used in positive statements whereas *any* is used in negative statements and questions.
* A verb is a 'doing' word.
* The subject of a sentence is the person or thing that does the action.

What is English really like?

66 English is illogical and irregular and it follows no rules."

What are the rules of English? How does tense relate to time? What's the difference between *courage* and *bravery*? Is written English the same as spoken English? How can we explain to students how English works? Can we make useful generalisations?

How do people learn English?

66 Learning a language is a question of imitating correct forms."

Does such imitation always produce correct English sentences?

Discover English challenges myths, preconceived ideas and intuitions about language by raising awareness of these and other questions about the language. Teachers who understand the language can help their learners by giving accurate and informed explanations. The exercises in the first part of the book will sensitise you to the language you are teaching or learning. The commentary in the second part of the book explore the teaching implications of these insights about language.

To the teacher, trainee or advanced student using the book independently

You can work through the book in any order. Choose the topics that interest or perplex you. Whenever you can, discuss the exercises with colleagues and fellow students. Work through the exercises first, and make a note of your answers before you look at the commentaries and compare. The commentaries provide informed views rather than 'correct' answers. We have given top priority to the teaching implications of the points explored in the exercises and we have made generalisations to help teachers rather than to establish abstract rules.

To the teacher trainer

You can use this book as a resource and choose the topics that most interest you and your trainees. Wherever possible, we recommend working through the exercises in a group because the discussion and feedback sessions will be a useful way to raise awareness. Many of the exercises challenge conventional views of language so you should be prepared for resistance and for a variety of views to be aired. Given the open-ended nature of awareness work, the commentaries are offered as an aid rather than as correct answers.

References

We found these books useful in writing and revising the material and suggest that those asterisked may prove useful to advanced learners and to trainees preparing to teach English for the first time.

Arndt, V. et al 2000 *Alive to Language* (Cambridge University Press)
Cowie, A.P. and Mackin R. 1993 *The Oxford Dictionary of English Idioms* (Oxford University Press)
*Leech, G. 1987 *Meaning and the English Verb*, 2nd edition (Longman)
Lewis, M. 1986 *The English Verb* (Language Teaching Publications)
Sinclair, J. (ed.) 1993 *Collins Cobuild English Grammar* (Collins)
*Swan, M. 2004 *Practical English Usage* (Oxford University Press)
The Longman Dictionary of Contemporary English, revised edition 1989 (Longman)
Teacher's resource books which make use of language awareness techniques:
Frank, C. and Rinvolucri, M. 1991 *Grammar in Action Again!*, 2nd rev. edition (Prentice Hall)
Morgan, J. and Rinvolucri, M. 1986 *Vocabulary* (Oxford University Press)
Language practice books for learners which make use of language awareness techniques:
Couter, R. et al 2000 *Exploring Grammar in Context* (Cambridge University Press)
Hall, N. and Shepheard, J. 1991 *The Anti-grammar Grammar Book* (Longman)
Woods, E. and Macleod, N. 1990 *Using English Grammar* (Prentice Hall)

Useful websites

http://www.onestopenglish.com
http://www.hltmag.co.uk
http://www.developingteachers.com
http://www.bbc.co.uk/worldservice/learningenglish
http://www.etprofessional.com
http://www.iatefl.org

Macmillan Books for Teachers

Welcome to the Macmillan Books for Teachers series. These books are for you if you are a trainee teacher, practising teacher or teacher trainer. They help you to:

- develop your skills and confidence
- reflect on what you do and why you do it
- inform your practice with theory
- improve your practice
- become the best teacher you can be

The handbooks are written from a humanistic and student-centred perspective. They offer:

- practical techniques and ideas for classroom activities
- key insights into relevant background theory
- ways to apply techniques and insights in your work

The authors are teachers and trainers. We take a 'learning as you go' approach in sharing our experience with you. We help you reflect on ways you can facilitate learning, and bring your personal strengths to your work. We offer you insights from research into language and language learning and suggest ways of using these insights in your classroom. You can also go to http://www.onestopenglish.com and ask the authors for advice.

We encourage you to experiment and to develop variety and choice, so that you can understand the how and why of your work. We hope you will develop confidence in your own teaching and in your ability to respond creatively to new situations.

Adrian Underhill

Titles in the series

⊕ Exercises

Unit 1 Myths and misconceptions

1 The English language

A Comment on the opening statement in the light of the extracts 1–3 that follow.

I want my students to speak only the best English so I encourage them to read only the classics of English literature.

> 1
> I've tried a long time, and 't'nt got better. But thou'st right; 't might mak fok talk even of thee.
>
> 2
> The robbery at the bank had not languished before, and did not cease to occupy a front place in the attention of the Principal of the establishment now.

Charles Dickens, *Hard Times*

> 3
> If a Struldbrugg happens to marry one of his own kind, the marriage is dissolved of course by the courtesy of the kingdom as soon as the younger of the two comes to be fourscore.

Jonathan Swift, *Gulliver's Travels*

B Comment on these statements:

1 I'm an Englishman and I'm proud of our great and ancient language. We must fight against these modern colloquialisms and the corruption of our language by vulgar Americanisms. Let's keep our language pure.

2 The use of *hopefully* except with the meaning *in a hopeful way* is unacceptable. So also is the use of *due to* in such public announcements as *Play stopped due to rain* and *Trains delayed, due to ice on the rails*. The phrase should be used only when preceded by a noun or noun plus linking verb, as in *The stoppage was due to rain*.

3 *Some* is only used in positive statements whereas *any* is used in negative statements and questions.

4 A verb is a doing word.

5 The subject of a sentence is the person or thing that does the action.

6 The past tenses always refer to the past, eg *He was going to the match*.

7 Countable nouns refer to things which you can count (eg *chairs, books, apples*) whereas uncountable nouns refer to things which you cannot count (eg *rice, soap, money*).

8 *will* is never used in clauses which begin with *when, after, before* or *as soon as*.

9 People who speak such varieties of English as Nigerian English, Jamaican English and Malaysian English should be taught to use Standard English at all times.

10 *Kid* is not an acceptable substitute for *child* just as *fag* and *kip* are not acceptable substitutes for *cigarette* and *sleep*.

11 I believe in plain English. A house is always a house and never a dwelling. A sentence is always a sentence and never a speech act.

12 I can understand my teacher very easily but when I talk English to people in the street they speak too quickly.

13 I've been teaching English for thirty years and I know what I'm doing. I teach only what has been judged by time and literature to be correct.

14 Only speakers of educated, standard southern English should teach English to foreigners. People who speak a dialect teach incorrect English.

15 A good English speaker never uses slang so I never allow my students to use English slang.

2 Learning English

A Comment on the statement in the light of the evidence (1–5).

English is a stupid language. It is illogical and irregular and it follows no rules.

1 swimming / dining / sinned / lined / hated / baited / getting / greeting

2 It's hot, isn't it? / She's fat, isn't she? / You didn't come, did you? / I've won, haven't I? / She'll come, won't she? / He wasn't happy, was he? / The bus is late, isn't it? / Mary had finished, hadn't she?

3 He bought it. / She grew it. / He brought it. / I showed them. / He wanted it. / I cleaned it. / I blamed them. / He cheated them. / I went there. / He sold it.

4 Have you got any money? / Have you got some money? / Give me some books. / Give me any books. / We haven't got any more. / We haven't got some more.

5 Well, they're very different, aren't they ... you know ... one's a sort of personal view and one is statistics ... it's interesting ... the one about the girl whose cousin 'had to get married' in 1960 and the difference when she ... 25 years later had a baby without being married ... I mean ... I think there's been a terrific shift in attitudes in that time ... I don't know if it's true of everywhere in the country ... I think if we live in the South East ... there's a ... a sort of... belief that people are changing everywhere.★

B Comment on the statement in the light of the evidence (1–3).

Learning a language is a question of imitating correct forms.

1 *Teacher:* We're having a test today.
  Pupil: Please sir, can I be excused? I'm having a bad headache.

2 *Teacher:* Have you ever been to Manchester?
  Pupil: Yes, I've been there last week.

3 *Teacher:* When will you do it?
  Pupil: I will do it when I will get home tonight.

★ Extract from Hopwood, T. and Rushton, R. 1990 *Heinemann Integrated Skills Advanced* (*Unit 9*, p 86.)

2

C   What contradictions are involved in these statements?

1   I will always insist that the pupils who I teach will follow the rules of the language so that they will learn to always speak correctly. I make sure that they always use 'shall' with 'I', that they always use 'whom' when the accusative form is required, that they never split an infinitive and that they never use a preposition to end a sentence with.

2   As I inculcated my amanuensis the sole bona fide mode of indoctrinating a language is to imbibe ten exotic words before retiring to somnambulance each evening. If you do not employ exotic words people deem you to be inerudite in the language.

D   Comment on the following statements.

1   You don't need a teacher to learn a foreign language. All you need is a grammar book and a dictionary.

2   You don't need a teacher to learn a foreign language. All you need is to read books written in the language and to listen to native speakers speaking it.

3   Constant repetition of correct forms is the key to learning a foreign language because it enables the learner to develop correct habits.

4   If you learn the grammar of English you will be able to speak the language well.

5   If you learn the grammar well you will automatically transfer listening and reading skills from your first language.

6   Listening skills and reading skills are very similar so if you teach learners reading skills they will be able to use them as listening skills too.

7   It's important to insist that learners of a language speak with the same correctness as we'd expect when they're writing.

8   As the grammar of good spoken English and of good written English are the same you can help learners to improve their spoken English by giving them lots of written grammar practice.

9   The teacher should always correct pronunciation errors or else the students will develop bad pronunciation.

10   I don't think he's a good teacher. Every time I walk past his classroom the students seem to be sitting in groups making a noise.

3   Terminology

In this book an attempt has been made to minimize the use of linguistic terminology. However, sometimes terms are used which may be useful and which are commonly used in books on language. As a preparation for meeting these terms, do the following exercises and then check the commentary before going on to Unit 2.

It might be a good idea to come back and do the relevant exercises in this section again if when you meet any of these terms you do not understand them. It might also be useful to revise the whole section when you have completed all the units in the book.

A   Look at the examples of the use of grammatical terms below and then complete the statements about them.

1 **Form** v **function**

Examples

The verb in the sentence is in a continuous **form**.
The plural **form** of *knife* is *knives*.
Must never changes its **form**.

One of the **functions** of the present perfect tense is to indicate that an action or event in the past is relevant in the present.
The **function** of *I'm not absolutely sure about that* can be to express polite disagreement.
One of the **functions** of *will* is to promise something.

Statements

The form of a word or structure is the parti............... w........ in which it is repre............... in wri......... or spe........... .

The functions of a word or structure in an utterance are the rol... it pl..... in the utterance, the purp......... it is used to exp........... .

A word or structure can be in a particular .... even when it is in isolation but it can only have a .... if it is used in an utterance. For example, *was going* is in the past continuous ...., but it does not have a .... unless we use it in an utterance (eg *I was going to Rome but now I've decided to go to Paris instead*).

2 **Time reference** v **tense**

Examples

In the utterance *I have been to Rome*, *have been* is in the present perfect **tense** but it has past **time reference**.

A verb in the present continuous **tense** can have future **time reference** (eg *She is going to Rio for her holiday*).

Statement

The tense of a verb is the fo..... in which it is wri.......... or spo.......... whereas the time reference is the per.......... of ti..... (ie pa....., pre.........., or fut........) which the verb refers to in the utte.......... .

3 **Full** v **contracted**

Example

In some types of writing you should always use the **full** forms of verbs but in other types you should use **contracted** forms. You should not use **contracted** forms of verbs in an academic essay but you should use them in a letter to a good friend.

Statement

The .... form is *I have* and the .... form is *I've*.

4 **Formal** v **informal**

Examples

I am afraid that I must express some reservations is a very **formal** way of expressing disagreement whereas *you must be joking* is an **informal** way of expressing a similar function.

Full forms of verbs should be used in **formal** writing (eg academic essays, scientific reports, job applications) but contracted forms can be used in **informal** writing (eg letters to friends, notes, invitations to friends).

Statement
.... language is used in situations which are off.......... or se.......... or which involve communication with supe.......... or stra.......... whereas .... language is used in situations which are rel............ or cas........ or which involve communication between people who kn........ each other we...... .

5 **Acceptable v unacceptable**

Examples
Gonna might not be strictly correct but it is certainly **acceptable** in such utterances between good friends as *I'm gonna see him tomorrow.* However most people would find it **unacceptable** in an official speech.

The American spelling of *color* is now **acceptable** to most English people.

Statement
A form of a word or structure which is not normally considered to be cor........ can be acc.............. in certain situ.............. or to certain peo........ .

6 **Context v cotext**

Examples
The meaning of a word depends on its **context**. For example, *He hasn't started yet* can have many different interpretations depending on the topic and the setting of the conversation and the relationship between the speakers. It could, for example, mean: *Until now he has always started a match as a substitute player*, *He is still practising*, *He will do a lot better than this soon*, or *The lecture has not begun.*

To understand a word you also need to relate it to its **cotext**. You can appreciate the different meanings of *bed* in the following examples even if you do not know anything about the **contexts** in which they were used.
I'm tired. I'm going to bed.
Put the seeds in that bed over there.

Statement
The .... of a word or utterance consists of the .... which come be.......... and af..... it, whereas the .... consists of the s................ in which it is used.

B Match the definitions 1–8 to the linguistic terms in **bold** type in (a)–(h).

1 It refers to the actual expressions used to communicate particular functions or notions.
2 A concept or area of meaning.
3 An utterance or series of related utterances used to achieve a specific intended outcome.
4 A word or group of words used with specific meaning in a particular context.
5 It refers to the ability of one expression to replace another without any loss of meaning or grammaticality.
6 Communication between people involving the use of language.
7 Relating to the expression of meaning.
8 The actual object, idea, emotion, etc referred to by a lexical item.

(a) It is important that students take part in **interaction** in the language they are learning.

(b) *How about, Would you like to, We'd be happy if* and *Why don't you* can all be **exponents** of the function of invitation.

(c) When Sheila says, 'I'm going. I can't put up with his bad temper any more' *put up with* is an expression consisting of three words but it is only one **lexical item**.

(d) A notional approach concentrates on teaching learners how to express different aspects of the main concepts represented by the language, such as the **notions** of time, duration, space and quantity.

(e) *Reach* and *arrive* are very similar in meaning but they are not completely **interchangeable**.

(f) Her three confident answers to his questions were all part of a **speech act** aiming to persuade him to loan her the money.

(g) It is important that students can give a **semantic** interpretation of the utterance and not just be able to analyse it grammatically.

(h) You can show students the **referent** of *table, window* or *chair* but it is more difficult to teach them the referents of *respect* or *duty*.

Unit 2 **Common areas of difficulty**

1 Basic grammatical terms

A Classify these words into nouns, pronouns, adjectives, adverbs, conjunctions or prepositions. (If you already know the basic word classes, as found in most dictionaries, leave out the exercise.)

1	window	9	strongly	17	because
2	happiness	10	grin	18	gargoyle
3	meander	11	him	19	ennui
4	blue	12	iridescent	20	malinger
5	if	13	avoid	21	although
6	under	14	comatose	22	by
7	our	15	courageously	23	aberration
8	be	16	cogitate	24	they

B **1** Divide this list of nouns into three categories, giving a heading to each.

elephant hope September delay Diana humour car marmalade radio Poland truth telegraph pole mirror oak excitement

2 Divide this list of nouns into two groups, giving a heading to each.

raisin cake carton shop nut milk rice spaghetti sugar money boot pot butter pound teaspoon water

C Divide the verbs in these utterances into two categories, stating reasons for your allocation.

1 You've finished your tea.
2 They are eating cake.
3 They are eating at home.
4 She wants to watch TV.
5 I'm going to bed.
6 I'm repairing the car.
7 Cortez conquered Mexico.
8 Many leading politicians have died violently.
9 I can't think clearly!
10 I hate this exercise!

D **1** Identify the **direct objects** in this passage.

I was hungry after walking a long way and looked round for a restaurant. It took me quite a while to find the only one in town and fortunately it was open. I asked the waitress a few questions about the menu. She gave me some rather hazy replies and so I decided to order something safe – a vegetable casserole. She brought me a beef casserole instead, much to my annoyance. I don't normally eat red meat and so I asked her to take it back.

She came back full of apologies and offered me a cheese salad as there was no vegetable casserole left. An elderly lady at the next table had just demolished the last portion! I was so hungry that I accepted the cheese salad but it wasn't very appetizing. Contrary to my usual custom I didn't leave this waitress a tip!

2 Identify the verbs with two objects.
3 Give some more examples of such verbs and explain why not all verbs can have two objects.

E   Why are these utterances wrong?

1   ✗ He got up early because his work.
2   ✗ He gave she a present.
3   ✗ They ate a quickly breakfast before going out.
4   ✗ During they were eating, the doorbell rang.
5   ✗ 'There's something blocking the road.' 'OK, we'll avoid.'
6   ✗ He learns very slow.
7   ✗ They gives her a lot of help.
8   ✗ I want to listen the news at 9 o'clock.

F   Why do these nonsense sentences **sound** acceptable?

1   He crattled his splot and scrot out a neelying groal.
2   They strentered folicly until a magan veened to famble them.

G   Look these words up in a dictionary. How does the dictionary deal with them?

sits	was	swore	swam
women	loaves	sung	loafs
spoken	bought	cats	fishes
talked	driven	drew	burnt

H   **1**   In the following extract, find examples of:

(a) a ditransitive verb (a verb with two objects)   (e) a proper noun
(b) an abstract noun   (f) an intransitive verb
(c) an uncountable noun   (g) a conjunction
(d) an irregular verb form (past simple or past participle)   (h) an adverb

If children come to feel that the universe does not make sense, it may be because the language we use to talk about it does not seem to make sense, or at least because there are contradictions between the universe as we experience it and as we talk about it.

One of the main things we try to do in schools is to give children a tool – language – with which to learn, think, and talk about the world they live in. Or rather, we try to help them refine the tool they already have. We act as if we thought this tool of language were perfect, and children had only to learn to use it correctly, ie as we do. In fact, it is in many ways a most imperfect tool. If we were more aware of its imperfections, of the many ways in which it does not fit the universe it attempts to describe, of the paradoxes and contradictions built into it, then we could warn the children, help them see where words and experience did not fit together, and perhaps show them ways of using language that would to some extent rise above its limitations.

Look at adjectives – some are, so to speak, absolute: round, blue, green, square. But many others are relative: long, short; thin, thick; heavy, light; high, low; near, far; easy, hard; loud, soft; hot, cold. None of these have any absolute meaning. Long and short only mean longer and shorter than something else. But we use these words as if they were absolutes. In fact, there must be many times when a child hears a particular thing called long one day and short the next, or hot one day and cold the next. We use words as if they were fixed in meaning, but we keep changing the meanings. The soup that has become cold is still too hot for the baby. The short pencil today is the long pencil tomorrow. The big kitty's name is Midnight; but don't be rough with him, he's too little. Horses are big animals; see the little horsie (three times the size of the child). How big you've grown; you can't have that, you're too little. Children adjust to this kind of confusion; but is it an intellectually healthy and useful adjustment, or just a kind of production strategy? Would it be useful to talk to first-graders about why we call a certain mountain small and a certain kitten big? Or is this easy stuff for them?

The conventional teaching of grammar adds to the confusion. We talk about, and use, nouns and adjectives as if they were very different, but in fact they are often much alike. A green ball, a green top, a green bicycle, and a green stuffed animal are alike in that they are green (adjective) and that they are toys (noun). When we call them green we mean they are members of a class that have in common the colour green. When we call them toys we mean that they are members of a class that have in common the fact that children play with them. Why should a child be expected to feel that there is something very different about these classes? Why is the green-ness of a ball different from the ball-ness of a ball? I don't feel the difference. They are both ways of saying something about the object. We tell children that the distinction between one part of speech and another is a matter of meaning, when it really has to do with the way we fit them into sentences.

John Holt (1969), *How Children Fail* (Pelican)

2 Discuss this 'child's eye' depiction of the illogicalities of grammatical categories and meanings. Do you think that young children will find terms like *conjunction* and *preposition* easier or more difficult to understand than *adjective* and *noun*? How can a teacher help a young child to overcome these difficulties? Do you think a teacher of English as a second or foreign language is likely to face similar difficulties with her learners? Give reasons for your answer.

2 Forms and functions

What do the utterances in each of these groups have in common? What distinguishes the sentences within each group from each other? (If necessary, check in the commentary after doing exercise **A** to see whether you are on the right track.)

A 1 Willy smokes.
2 Fred's a slow worker.
3 Aggie used to drink.
4 Joe's in the habit of talking in his sleep.
5 He's always making that mistake.

B 1 Pollution is getting worse.
2 It's raining.
3 I'm going out tonight.
4 He's always dropping ash on the carpet.

C 1 Simmer for 15 minutes over a low heat.
2 Come again soon.
3 Halt!
4 Give us this day our daily bread.

       5 Don't mention it.

       6 When in Rome, do as the Romans do.

D   1 See you!

       2 The Queen is due to arrive at 4 pm.

       3 He's about to arrive.

       4 The train leaves at 3 pm.

       5 Willy's going to be an engine driver.

       6 He's taking his finals in June.

       7 I'll be 64 next birthday.

E   1 If I were you, I'd stay.

       2 It's time you went home.

       3 Wish you were here!

       4 If only he had worked harder!

       5 Suppose someone had seen us.

F   1 I doubt if he'll come.

       2 It might rain.

       3 There's a 50–50 chance of play today.

       4 He's bound to turn up.

       5 She's likely to pass her test.

3 Tense and time

A **1** These statements were all made by the same person. Put them into chronological order as far as you can.

    (a) We're going to live in Liverpool.

    (b) After we've lived in Liverpool for a few years, we'll move back to Wigan.

    (c) We live in Wigan.

    (d) We lived in Bradford for 5 years.

    (e) We were going to move to London in 1983 but my job there fell through.

    (f) By the time we move to Liverpool, we'll have spent 3 years in Wigan.

    (g) We lived in Manchester for a while before we moved to Bradford.

How were you able to do this? What were the essential clues?

2 This diagram represents time in a schematic way. Assuming that the speaker is at point 1 (the present), allocate each of the seven statements (a)–(g) to a number on the diagram.

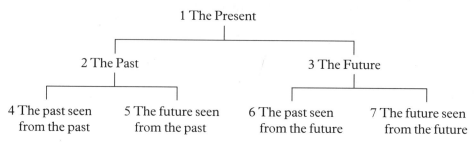

1 The Present

2 The Past

3 The Future

4 The past seen from the past

5 The future seen from the past

6 The past seen from the future

7 The future seen from the future

B   Comment on the validity of these statements.

1 Present tenses are always used to express present time in English.
2 Past tenses are always used to express past time in English.
3 The English tense system is based on, and can be equated with, the Latin tense system.
4 Different peoples perceive time differently, and these differences are reflected in the tense systems of their languages.
5 Different languages have developed different ways of referring to concepts of time.
6 The verb is the main marker of time in an English sentence.

4   Questions

A   Divide these utterances into two broad categories; state what your criteria are.

1 Where's my pen?
2 When is the train due in?
3 Are you listening?
4 How far is it to London?
5 Isn't that my pen?
6 Why haven't you done your homework?
7 That's not your pen, is it?
8 Would you like coffee or tea?
9 Would you like some more wine?
10 What's the time?
11 You've been to Liverpool before, haven't you?
12 How are you?

B   Divide these questions into categories; state what your criteria are.

1 Is the TV still on?
2 Haven't you finished eating yet?
3 Can you lend me £5?
4 That's not Helen, is it?
5 Have you locked the back door?
6 Has someone opened this letter?
7 It isn't raining again, is it?
8 Do you mind if I smoke?
9 Was Mike at the party last night?
10 Shall I open the door for you?
11 This can't possibly be right, can it?
12 Do you want some more cake?
13 You have posted the letter, haven't you?
14 Nice day, isn't it?

C   Account for these learners' errors.

1 ✗ Does he plays tennis?
2 ✗ Am not I right?
3 ✗ Did you went to town last week?
4 ✗ How often play you tennis?
5 ✗ Do you can play chess?
6 ✗ You don't like carrots, like you?
7 ✗ Shall you open the door for me, please?
8 ✗ We'd better go now, betn't we?

D   Look at these conversational exchanges and explain the misunderstandings.

1 *A:* How do you do?
   B: I do very well, thank you.
2 *A:* How are you?
   B: How are you?
3 *A:* Can you open the door?
   B : (*not moving*) Yes, I can.
4 *A:* Do you read a newspaper?
   B: No, I have my tea.
5 *A:* You've finished that work, haven't you?
   B : (*impatiently*) Of course I have.

E   Match each of the questions 1–10 with a function from the list (a)–(j).

Questions

1   What time is it?
2   Is that a stoat or a weasel?
3   You're back rather early, aren't you?
4   What do you mean *early*?
5   *Must* you play your harmonica in the living-room?
6   Shall I do that for you?
7   Would you mind holding this for a moment?
8   Why are you late?
9   What sort of car was he driving?
10   What do you think of the new goalkeeper?

Functions

(a) asking someone to distinguish between alternatives
(b) expressing incredulity
(c) offering assistance
(d) asking for assistance
(e) asking for information
(f) expressing irritation
(g) asking for an opinion
(h) expressing mild surprise
(i) asking for an explanation
(j) asking for a description

F   Food for thought.

1   Why do you think learners of English often find it difficult to form interrogatives and to ask questions correctly?
2   In the light of your conclusions after the preceding exercises, why do you think it is important for a language teacher to distinguish between the terms **question** and **interrogative**?

5   Future time

A   In many grammars and coursebooks, the future is dealt with as a tense, formed by *shall/will* + infinitive. It is often known as the **pure future**. Which of the following examples could be described as **pure future**? What do *shall* or *will* add to the meaning in the other examples?

1   Don't worry! I'll help you with your homework.
2   My brother *will* talk with his mouth full.
3   Pass the mustard, will you?
4   Shall I open the door for you?
5   I'll see you at the party tonight.
6   Shall we go for a drink?
7   Trespassers will be prosecuted.
8   Boys will be boys.
9   Do you think Liverpool will win on Saturday?
10   You shall do as I tell you!
11   Summer will soon be over.

B Below are examples of different ways of expressing future meaning. Provide a context for each example. Then comment on why there is no standardized future **tense** in English.

1 She'll be 83 next July.
2 *A:* I'm just going down to the village.
   B: Will you be going near the Post Office?
3 *A:* I've lost my wallet again!
   B: What are you going to do about it?
4 There's going to be a crash on that bend soon.
5 What are you doing this evening?
6 We hope to go abroad next year.
7 John is about to resign from his job.
8 You never know what might happen.
9 The film starts at 8.15.

C Which of these statements about *shall* and *will* do you accept?

1 *Shall* is never used these days.
2 *Shall* ought always to be used with the first person and *will* with the second and third persons.
3 In conversation, the difference between *shall* and *will* has become unimportant (in most cases).
4 *Shall* ought always to be taught as it is strictly correct in certain cases.
5 There is no real need to teach *shall*.

Which statements could also apply to *should* and *would*?

D Which way of expressing the future would you teach first. Why?

6 Voice

A Where might these statements be found? What do you notice about the verb forms?

On parle français.   Se habla español.
Man spricht Deutsch.   English spoken.

B Provide appropriate contexts for the following utterances. Give reasons for your conclusions.

1 Customers are asked to use the baskets provided.
2 My car's been stolen!
3 200 people are reported to have died in the riots.
4 It's being repaired.
5 You have been warned!
6 Trespassers will be prosecuted.
7 Chris Hani assassinated.

C Can you improve this passage, focusing on the verb forms?

> *Oxygen*
> Joseph Priestley prepared oxygen for the first time in 1774. He prepared it by heating mercuric oxide, but nowadays we produce it commercially in large quantities by a process which we call fractional distillation. Both air and water contain it. Plants also give it off in their respiratory process.

D This exercise is typical of many coursebook treatments of the passive. What will learners learn from doing it? What will they not learn?

> **Make these sentences passive.**
>
> Example: *John wrote that letter.*
> *That letter was written by John.*
>
> 1 The cow jumped over the moon.
> 2 Willy ate his sister's porridge.
> 3 Shakespeare wrote Hamlet.
> 4 Somebody broke into our house last night.
> 5 Koala bears eat eucalyptus leaves.
> 6 The Queen has just opened Parliament.

E Compare the effect of active v passive in these utterances.

1 They went home as there was nothing more to do.
    They went home as there was nothing more to be done.
2 There's nothing to see in Scotland.
    There was no one to be seen on the streets.

F What do the verbs in these utterances have in common?

1 He was deemed to be the best man for the job.
2 She is reputed to be rich.
3 I was born in the North of England.
4 His past is shrouded in mystery.
5 The tennis tournament was rained off.

G What is the effect of the use of the passive in these mini-dialogues?

1 *Soldier:* Sorry I'm late, sir. It wasn't my fault.
    Officer: You've been warned about lateness before.
    Soldier: I know, sir.
2 *Interviewer:* Can you give an undertaking to keep inflation down?
    Prime Minister: It is to be hoped that it will not exceed 10 per cent this year.
3 *Interviewer:* And where is the General now?
    Spokesman: He is believed to be abroad.
4 *Professor:* Have you read *The Unbearable Lightness of Being*?
    Student: No, but I've read some of V.S. Naipaul's other books.
    Professor: But *The Unbearable Lightness of Being* was written by Milan Kundera.
5 *Willy:* What's happened to Joe?
    Fred: He's been taken to hospital.

H Why is the passive so common in texts such as these?

1

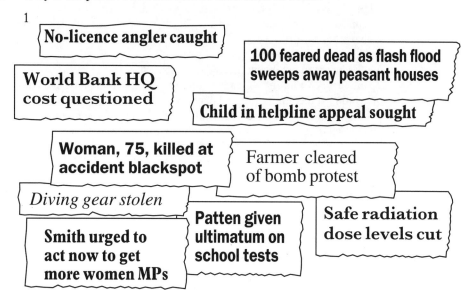

No-licence angler caught

World Bank HQ cost questioned

100 feared dead as flash flood sweeps away peasant houses

Child in helpline appeal sought

Woman, 75, killed at accident blackspot

Farmer cleared of bomb protest

Diving gear stolen

Patten given ultimatum on school tests

Safe radiation dose levels cut

Smith urged to act now to get more women MPs

2

DELICIOUS DISCOVERIES
No 1: Beenleigh Blue cheese

Beenleigh Blue was first made only 10 years ago. The milk is from sheep that graze the ancient steep pastures along the banks of the Dart estuary in May and June. After that, mystically, the character of the milk changes and Robin Congdon, the sole producer of Beenleigh, stops production. Only 1500 cheeses are made each year. They are turned six times by hand and kept for that first day at 22 degrees to allow the bacteria to continue working. They are then salted and spiked to let in the air which will mark out the distinctive blue. The cheeses are then matured and wrapped in foil for at least four months, though the flavours improve for eight or nine months. By then, the taste will be steely blue, tangy, rich and, unusually, slightly sweet.

Beenleigh is unpasteurised and organic. It is best eaten on its own as an imperial finale to a meal. The best, probably by now at their peak, may still be found in specialist cheese shops. The first of this year's cheeses will be available from late September.

Drew Smith, *Observer Magazine*, 25 April 1993

3

When we introduced the subject of alternating current we said that the very great use made of a.c. supply systems is due to the ease with which an a.c. supply can be stepped up or down in voltage. To do this we use a *static transformer*. This device transforms low-voltage energy into high-voltage energy or vice versa.

Transformers are also required for the operation of most luminous discharge tubes and for bell systems in the home; they are found in radio and television equipment, with several different types often used in the same circuit; telephone systems use large numbers of transformers, as does X-ray equipment: so that we might say that where electricity is used, transformers are used too.

Essentially a transformer consists of two independent electric circuits linked with a common magnetic circuit. In particular, it usually consists of two coils or windings of

> insulated copper wire around a laminated iron core. An alternating magnetic flux is produced in this iron core when an alternating current passes through the insulated conductors. In operation, an a.c. supply is connected to one winding which thereby becomes the primary winding: the other winding, to which the load is connected, is called the secondary winding.
>
> The magnetic flux in the magnetic circuit formed by the iron core links the turns of the primary and the secondary windings. If this flux is the same for each of the two windings, the e.m.f. induced per turn must be the same in each winding, so that the total induced e.m.f. in each winding will be proportional to the number of turns on that winding.

J. McAllister and G. Madanna (1976), *English for Electrical Engineers* (Longman)

I Compare these pairs of sentences:

1 He's just had his watch repaired.
He's just repaired his watch.

2 Where can I get this film developed?
Where can this film be developed?

3 He's just had three teeth out.
Three of his teeth have just been taken out.

J Try this exercise and comment on its effectiveness from a teacher's point of view.

Complete each sentence on the lines of the example.

Do you repair you own car or *do you have it repaired?*

1 Do you cut your own hair or …
2 Do you do your own gardening or …
3 Do you fetch your own newspaper or ….
4 Do you make your dresses yourself or …
5 Do you clean your car yourself or …

---

7 Conditionals and hypothetical meaning

A Provide a possible context for each of these utterances and comment on the verb forms in *italics*. The first two have been done as examples.

1 If only it *would rain*!
This might be said by a farmer whose crops are threatened by a drought. It obviously hasn't rained for a long time. The verb form *would rain* emphasizes the hypothetical nature of the wish, which refers to the future.

2 If only it *rained* more often!
This might also be said by a farmer whose crops don't get enough rain. He seems to live in an area where the annual rainfall is low, and the verb form *rained*, in this context, is not past in meaning, but refers to the present in a hypothetical way.

3 I wish you *were* here.
4 If I *were* a rich man, I wouldn't have to work hard.

5 If I *had* a hammer, I'd hammer in the morning.
6 It's time you *washed* your feet.
7 Suppose you *were* in my position, what would you do?
8 *Had* you *arrived* earlier, you'd have had enough to drink.
9 He speaks as if he *knew* everything about cars.
10 Would you mind if I *smoked*?

What do the utterances have in common with each other in terms of meaning?

B Which of these utterances might apply to (a) a good student, (b) a lazy student and (c) an ex-student?

1 If he worked hard, he'd pass.
2 If he had worked hard, he would have passed.
3 He'll pass if he works hard.

C Group these utterances according to the function of *would* in each.

1 He told me he would pay me back.
2 I wish it would rain.
3 Would you mind helping me?
4 It would be difficult to refuse such an offer if it came.
5 *A:* I've forgotten my keys.
  B: You would!
6 You would do well to take his advice!
7 Queen Victoria would seldom smile.
8 I'd be grateful if you would stop blowing smoke in my eyes.
9 I was hoping you would come.
10 Would that you were here!

In the light of your observations, do you think it is useful to talk about a conditional **tense**? or about conditional **sentences**?

D Divide sentences 1–13 into *three* groups for teaching purposes. State your criteria. Providing a context for each utterance may help you to arrive at your decisions.

1 I wish I had more time.
2 If you come tonight, you'll meet her.
3 If only I had worked harder!
4 You'll have an accident unless you slow down.
5 I'd take care if I were you.
6 There'll be no trouble provided you keep calm.
7 You'd do well to cut down your smoking.
8 There might never have been an accident if the road had been dry.
9 I'd feel better if I could lie down.
10 Without the millions invested by the oil companies, North Sea oil might never have been discovered.
11 Given a little luck, we'll succeed.
12 Should you change your mind, I'll be happy to hear from you.
13 Were you to have second thoughts, I'd be glad to re-open negotiations.

8   Functions

A   What are the possible functions of the words in *italics*?

1   I *have given* it to him.
2   (a) *How about* using glue? (b) *Let's go*.
3   The water *was heated* to a temperature of 80°C.
4   You are coming tonight, *aren't you*?
5   I showed him the book *so that he could* help me to solve the problem.
6   *Do you think you could find time* to look through this book?
7   He walked to the window *and* opened it as far as it would go.
8   I *meet* him next Tuesday.
9   It's not something I've had much experience in. *Nevertheless* I'll do it for you.
10   *The* house is for sale now.
11   *It's not only* the cost that is the problem; I just haven't got time.
12   *It* has been discussed many times before.
13   I *rang* him yesterday at ten.
14   He is *always* picking his nose.
15   He bought two books *and* three magazines.
16   *I'm not entirely sure that I agree*.

B   What is meant by *function* in **A**?

C   Look back at the 16 examples in **A** and use them to help you to write different definitions of the term *function*. Then place each example with one of your definitions.

D   What do you think is meant by *function* in *We must teach both the form and the function of structures*?

E   What is meant by *functional* in *The Functional Approach puts the emphasis on what is done through language*?

F   What is the function of the expressions in *italics*?

1   *A: Let's go* now.
    B: No way.
2   *A: I'm sure* their offer is a very fair one.
    B: No way.
3   *A: Would you like to* come in for a coffee?
    B: Thank you very much.
4   *A: Press* button A.
    B: Again?
5   *A: You* ought to *get out more.*
    B: Too true.

9   Teaching functions

A   **1**   What do the following utterances have in common?

(a)   I'm not quite sure I agree.
(b)   You could be right but I think …
(c)   That's your opinion, is it?
(d)   I would like to contest that point.
(e)   I disagree.

(f)   I don't think it's right …
(g)   I'm not so sure I would go along with you there.
(h)   Nonsense!
(i)   That's not true.
(j)   I'd like to express my disagreement …
(k)   That's all very well but …
(l)   On the contrary …
(m) No way.
(n)   I don't think I agree …

2 What are the main differences between the above utterances?
3 If you were going to teach the function of disagreement to a group of post-elementary adult learners which of the above utterances would you teach? How would you teach them?
4 List other exponents of the function of disagreement. Would you teach any of these to the group specified in 3 above?
5 What conclusions can you draw from questions 1–4 about the teaching of functions?

B   Two learners of English performed the following impromptu dialogue after being taught ways of complaining and apologizing.

A: Excuse me, would you mind turning down your radio?
B: Oh, I am terribly sorry. What can I possibly do to put it right?
A: I won't ask you again.
B: Not at all. I really must apologise.
A: I must warn you I won't tolerate it any more.
B: I'm so sorry.

1 What is wrong with the dialogue?
2 What faults in the teaching do you think might have been responsible for the learners producing such a faulty performance?
3 As a result of your analysis of this dialogue what would you say were the most important things to remember when teaching functions?

C   1 What is wrong with the following dialogue?

A: Please could you possibly lend me £5?
B: I'm broke.
A: How about lending me your car?
B: I wish I could but it's in the garage.
A: I'd be so grateful if you could find your way to lending me your pen for a minute.
B: No way!
A: Give me a cigarette.
B: If only I could.

2 What two functions are exemplified in the above dialogue?
3 What are the differences between the exponents of the two functions exemplified in the dialogue?
4 List other exponents of the two functions to teach to a lower intermediate class. For each exponent say what you think it would be important for the learner to learn about it.
5 What are your criteria for selecting these functions?

10 Reporting speech

A **1** Which of the functions listed below would be possible, as interpretations of the utterance in the cartoon?

> ordering cajoling begging reminding inviting persuading advising insisting requesting permitting recommending suggesting warning compelling intending approving threatening scolding

2 How might the boy in the picture be able to decide exactly what his mother means?
3 Now turn the same utterance into indirect (reported) speech, once for each of the functions you have chosen.

B Comment on this typical exercise for learners of English. What might they learn from doing it? What might they not learn?

> **Put the following into reported speech:**
> 1 'Go to your room and stay there till I call you!' he said.
> 2 'Finish your meat or there'll be no ice-cream,' she said.
> 3 'Don't spend all your money in one shop,' he said.
> 4 'Keep still,' he said, irritably.
> 5 'Wait here till the taxi arrives,' she said.
> 6 'Don't you dare run away again!' he said.
> 7 'Don't shoot, please,' he said in a quavering voice.
> 8 'Take your partners for the rumba,' the bandleader said.
> 9 'Listen to me, will you,' said the teacher curtly.
> 10 'Lead us not into temptation …' (The Lord's Prayer).
> 11 'We'll go tomorrow,' she said.
> 12 'They arrived this morning,' he said.

C **1** Comment on the writer's choice of direct or indirect speech in this newspaper extract.

Patten says tests will go ahead

THIS summer's national curriculum tests will go ahead, the Secretary of State for Education insisted yesterday, despite an opinion poll in yesterday's *Independent* showing that 62 per cent of parents think they should be abandoned, *writes Colin Hughes*.

John Patten said he could not afford to allow the Government's educational reforms to stall: "We are at a critical moment in the introduction of education reforms. It is extremely easy on the back of the [Newbury] by-election defeat to say we have to stop doing this or that or the other because clearly it has made us unpopular.

'You do not succeed in the process of reform by stopping. You simply fall off the bicycle, and you never get pedalling again,' he told the BBC Radio 4 *Today* programme.

The embattled minister recognises that testing of 14-year-olds will be patchy because of the teacher boycott, but he believes that some schools and teachers do want to do it. His officials pointed out that many primary schools had almost completed testing seven-year-olds anyway.

Sir Ron Dearing, chairman of the curriculum and assessment authorities, reiterated his view that evidence from the tests would help his review of the national curriculum, but he did not want to take sides 'in what has become an industrial relations issue'.

Sir Ron, speaking in London at the first consultation conference for his review of the curriculum, told teachers that he hoped the review would provide them with 'a better tool for their job'.

From The *Independent*, 11 May 1993

2 Are there any instances in the article where the conventional 'rules' of reported speech have been broken?

D What do exercises **A–C** above suggest to you about the teaching of direct or indirect speech when reporting?

11 Notions

A **1** What do the expressions in *italics* in the following sentences have in common?

(a) I'm going *for a* month.
(b) He's lived here *since* 1972.
(c) We waited *till* ten.
(d) Stay here *until* I come back.
(e) We had to wait a *long time*.
(f) He *was watching* television.
(g) We *had been waiting* for three hours when he arrived.
(h) *How long* did you stay there?
(i) We enjoyed *the day* immensely.
(j) We spent *a week* there.
(k) I *think* he's an honest man.

2 Explain when each of the expressions could be used, eg

(b) To refer to a period of time in the past from the date mentioned to a point of time established by the situation (ie now) or a previous utterance.
Always followed by an expression referring to a point of time.

3 Write down any other similar expressions you can think of and then either link them to explanations you have already given or, if this is not possible, give separate explanations for them.

B **1** What do the expressions in *italics* have in common?

(a) The lorry *moved slowly forward.*
(b) He has *gone* to Wigan.
(c) I just saw him *going into* that pub.
(d) He was *walking towards* Linton.
(e) He's *gone out.*
(f) He *ran away from* the fire.
(g) *Go* and *fetch* it.

2 Explain the use of the expressions in *italics*.
3 Write down any similar expressions you can think of and then comment on them.
4 Decide what aspects of the notion of movement you would teach to an elementary class and then for each aspect decide which actual expressions you would teach.

C **1** The following expressions can be used to communicate the notion of location.

here	outside	where	on
there	this	somewhere	in
inside	that	everywhere	

Use *inside, this* and *on* in sentences in which they communicate the notion of location.

2 What notion can all of the following expressions communicate?

next to	behind	beside
between	in front of	on top of

3 What notion can all of the following expressions communicate?

first	had left	later on
then	afterwards	before

D **1** What notions do the expressions in *italics* communicate?

(a) Do it *like this.*
(b) He ate so much *that he felt ill.*
(c) It's *not the same thing.*
(d) You can open the door *with* this key.
(e) *At the same time* the bomb went off.

2 For each notion that you have referred to in 1, list three other exponents (ie expressions which can communicate aspects of the notion) and comment on the differences (if any) between the three exponents.

E You have decided to teach the notion of **contrast** to an intermediate level class.

1 Which expressions/structures would you teach? Why?
2 Which order would you teach them in? Why?
3 Would you teach them together in the same teaching unit or separately? Why?
4 How would you teach them?

F Do you think it is a good idea to devise teaching units in which you teach a range of different expressions/structures which can be used to communicate aspects of the same notion? Give reasons for your opinion.

12 Modal meaning

A   Sort these sentences into (a) those in which the verb in *italics* carries its own meaning and (b) those in which the meaning of the verb is **modified** in some way.

1   Children *are* noisy.
2   The TV *is* broken.
3   The TV must *be* broken.
4   I *see* my doctor every Monday.
5   You ought to *see* him more often.
6   I'm afraid I *can't* see him any more often.
7   Joe *was* in London yesterday.
8   But he couldn't have *been*.
9   Why not? – Because I *saw* him in Liverpool.
10   He'll *be* 64 next birthday.
11   Will you *open* the door for me?
12   You'll have to *work*.
13   Do you think John is likely *to come*?
14   I think he might *come*.
15   But it's essential that he should *come*.
In what different ways are the meanings of the verbs in category (b) modified?

B   We often speak of degrees of likelihood in terms of percentages.

1   If 0 per cent = *out of the question* and 100 per cent = *absolute certainty*, allocate these utterances to points on the line above which you feel indicate correctly the degree of likelihood which they express. It will help if you think of an appropriate context for each utterance.

(a)   Willy is definitely in England.
(b)   Willy may be in England.
(c)   There's an even chance that Willy's in England.
(d)   Willy might be in England.
(e)   There's no way that Willy could be in England.
(f)   Willy's probably in England.
(g)   Willy must be in England.
(h)   Willy just might be in England.
(i)   I doubt if Willy's in England.
(j)   Willy may very well be in England.
(k)   Willy could be in England.
(l)   Willy is likely to be in England.
(m)   Perhaps Willy's in England.
(n)   Willy's almost certainly in England.
(o)   Willy ought to be in England.

2   Which of these would you teach first? Why?

C **1** What distinguishes these different ways of asking for permission from each other?

    (a) OK if I go home now?

    (b) Would you mind if I went home now?

    (c) Can I go home now?

    (d) May I go home now?

    (e) Do you think I might go home now?

    (f) Could I go home now?

2 Which of these would you teach first? Why?

D Explain the function of the words in *italics* in each utterance.

    1 It *may* rain this afternoon.

    2 Willy *could* run fast when he was a boy.

    3 *May* I ask a question?

    4 You *needn't* go if you don't want to.

    5 You *might have* told me you were coming.

    6 That *can't* be true!

    7 They *must* be away. The curtains are drawn.

    8 He was told he *could* re-sit the exam.

    9 I've failed!

      You *could* try again next year.

   10 I *must* go.

E Jot down three ways of expressing each of the following.

    1 possibility

    2 ability

    3 imposing obligations on others

    4 necessity

    5 annoyance at irritating habits.

F What is the difference (if any) between the verbs in *italics* in the following pairs of utterances?

    1 (a) I *could* swim well when I was a boy.

      (b) He *was able to* escape by climbing the prison wall.

    2 (a) You *mustn't* do that.

      (b) You *don't have to* do that.

    3 (a) He *should* see a doctor.

      (b) He *ought to* see a doctor.

    4 (a) You *needn't* come if you don't want to.

      (b) You *don't need to* come if you don't want to.

    5 (a) I *may* come.

      (b) I *might* come.

    6 (a) I *shall* do it.

      (b) I *will* do it.

    7 (a) I *used to* enjoy listening to stories.

      (b) When I was a boy, my grandfather *would* take me on his knee and tell me stories.

13 Auxiliary verbs

A What is the main difference in function between the verbs underlined once and those underlined twice?

1 He <u>has</u> <u><u>gone</u></u> to the cinema.
2 I <u>must</u> <u><u>get</u></u> some work done.
3 No, I <u>didn't</u> <u><u>see</u></u> him at the match.
4 <u>Have</u> you <u><u>met</u></u> him before?
5 I <u>was</u> <u><u>waiting</u></u> for him to come.
6 I <u>can</u> <u><u>see</u></u> him now.
7 I <u>am</u> <u><u>working</u></u> tonight. I'<u>ll</u> <u><u>ring</u></u> you tomorrow.

B What is the difference in function between the verbs in *italics* in (a) and (b)?

1 (a) I *am* English.
  (b) I *am* going there tonight.
2 (a) He *has* four sisters.
  (b) He *has* gone to bed.
3 (a) He *does* two hours homework every night.
  (b) *Does* he like children?

C **1** What are the similarities and the differences in function between the verbs underlined once and those underlined twice?

(a) <u><u>Can</u></u> you swim?
(b) <u><u>Did</u></u> you swim?
(c) You <u>must</u> go, <u><u>mustn't</u></u> you?
(d) You <u>are</u> going, <u><u>aren't</u></u> you?
(e) <u><u>Has</u></u> the milkman been yet?
    Yes, he <u>has</u>.
(f) You <u>ought</u> to go home now.
(g) <u><u>Shall</u></u> I tell him?
(h) He <u>doesn't</u> want to come.
(i) They <u>had</u> already finished.
(j) He <u><u>couldn't</u></u> do it.
    No, he <u><u>couldn't</u></u>.

2 List other verbs like those underlined twice.

D What are the differences in function between the three verbs in the sentence *He has had to have an operation*?

E The verbs in *italics* are auxiliary verbs. Explain their main functions.

1 *Did* you like him?
  Yes, I *did*.
2 I *don't* like chips.
  Don't you?
3 They *haven't* even started yet.
4 You've lost it, *haven't* you?
5 He *is* doing it tonight.
6 *Had* he already mentioned it to you?
7 They *are* coming, *aren't* they?
8 *Are* you listening?
  Yes, I *am*.
9 He *was* hoping to go to university, *wasn't* he?
10 *Haven't* they gone to Brighton?
  No. But they *did* last year though.

F **1** Fill in the blanks in the dialogue below with verbs.

Roy: _____(a) she wearing that red dress last night?
Sam: No, she _____(b). She _____ (c) bought a black one which _____ (d) even more attractive.

Roy: _____ (e) you dance with her?

Sam: Yes, I _____(f). Two or three times. But then so _____ (g) every other man at the party.

Roy: _____ (h) there any other attractive women at the party?

Sam: Yes, lots. But none of them _____ (i) what Mary has.

Roy: I _____ (j) hoping to take her to the dance like I _____ (k) last year but she _____ (l) already agreed to go with Ian.

2 For each verb that you have added say whether it is an auxiliary verb or not. If it is, describe its function.

14 *Have* and *be*

A 1 Ask the questions which might have prompted these answers. Use *have* in each question, except those marked with an asterisk.

  *(a) It rang when I was having a bath.
  *(b) I was having a bath when it rang.
   (c) No, I'm sorry, I haven't.
   (d) Yes, I did.
   (e) No, he hasn't, he's got three.
   (f) I had a boiled egg, two slices of toast and a cup of tea.
   (g) An Opel Kadett.
  *(h) I'm having a sit-down and a smoke.
   (i) No, never.
   (j) Yes, I'll be having one next month.
   (k) A boy.
   (l) Sorry, I don't carry matches.

2 Look at the form of the questions you have made. Any comments?

B Comment on the meanings of *be* and *have*.

1 He *is having* his tonsils out tomorrow.
2 Don't *be* cruel.
3 He *has* three cooked meals a day.
4 She's just *being* stupid.
5 *Have* a drink on me.
6 She's just *had* her hair permed.
7 Our house *is being* repainted.

C One of each of the following pairs is wrong or at least unlikely. Identify it and say why you think it is wrong or unlikely.

1 (a) Be careful!
  (b) Be handsome!
2 (a) Don't be late!
  (b) He's being late.
3 (a) She's being stubborn.
  (b) She's being beautiful.
4 (a) I'm having three sisters.
  (b) I'm having a bath.
5 (a) Have a cigarette!
  (b) Have a headache!
6 (a) We've just had tea.
  (b) We've just had a new car.
7 (a) Being British, we were readily accepted.
  (b) We're being French.
8 (a) She's got a brand new coat.
  (b) She's got her dinner at 8.30 every evening.
9 (a) I don't have coffee every day.
  (b) I don't always be stupid.

D   Divide these utterances into two categories according to how *have* and *be* are used.

1 He *has* a cup of tea every morning.
2 He *has* a cup of tea in his hand.
3 Her cat's just *had* kittens.
4 You*'re* stupid.
5 They *have* three children.
6 *Being* stupid, you wouldn't understand.
7 Walls *have* ears.
8 You're *being* stupid!
9 Can I *have* a look, please?
10 *Have* a good time!
11 *Be* a good boy!
12 *Have* a piece of chewing gum.
13 We *haven't* any apples.
14 He*'s* a careful driver.
15 I*'ve* never *had* malaria.

E   In which of these utterances do *be* and *have* function as auxiliaries?

1 He *was* born in 1940.
2 *Having* seen *The Mousetrap*, I don't know why it's so popular.
3 He*'s*[1] just *been*[2] to London.
4 *Being* bright, he understood.
5 Our car*'s*[1] *being*[2] repaired.
6 Do you always *have* a shower before breakfast?
7 *Have*[1] you *had*[2] lunch yet?
8 He told her to *be* sensible.
9 What *have* you got in your hand?
10 Don't *be* obstructive!

F   **1**   *We shouldn't teach* have got (*eg* She's got one) *as it's too colloquial.* Discuss.

2   How did this mistake arise?
A: Don't be silly!
B: I don't!

3   And this one?
A: Where are my keys?
B: I haven't them.

4   What are the implications of these exercises for the teaching of *be* and *have*?

15 Comparisons

A   What do the following have in common? What distinguishes them?

1 The Nile is longer than the Zambezi.
2 *The Times* is a newspaper with a long tradition whereas the *Sun* is relatively new.
3 Black coal is usually found a long way below the Earth's surface; brown coal, on the other hand, is generally found on the surface.
4 Willy is not as bright as his brother.
5 Maggie didn't like the flat she was living in. She moved to a different one.
6 His hair is the same colour as mine.
7 I wish you'd speak more clearly!
8 He's less of an extrovert than his brother.
9 More motorists are in the Automobile Association than any other British motoring organization.
10 I eat more than I should.
11 I hope you'll be as happy as we are.
12 The more, the merrier.
13 It's as cold as ice out there.
14 You can't do better than your best.

B **1** The following is a textbook exercise on comparatives and superlatives. What does it practise and what does it leave out?

> **Choose the correct comparative or superlative form of one of these adjectives or adverbs to complete each sentence.**
>
> | fast far difficult high old heavy beautiful careful obedient bad |
>
> (a) An elephant is ____ than a hippopotamus.
> (b) Chinese is a ____ language to learn than Spanish.
> (c) Henry drives ____ than his brother.
> (d) Henry is ____ than his brother.
> (e) Drive ____ or we'll be late.
> (f) Dogs are generally ____than cats.
> (g) Mont Blanc is the ____ peak in the Alps.
> (h) Many people think that Paris is the ____ city in the world.
> (i) It is ____ from London to Edinburgh than from London to Brussels!
> (j) His condition is gradually getting ____.

2 What *rules* useful to learners of English can be generalized from these examples?

16 Tense and function 1

A Write down the verbs in each of the following utterances. For each verb name its tense and describe its function(s).

1 When they got to the station the train had already gone.
2 I was walking along Church Street when I saw Mary.
3 The programme will have finished by the time you have finished making the coffee.
4 You're too late. He's just gone home.
5 I see Bill got arrested again yesterday.
6 He walked to work every day when he worked at the station in 1968.
7 When he comes I will let you know.
8 *Passenger:* Which platform does the London train leave from?
   Rail worker (pointing to a train): It's just gone.
9 I've been waiting here for thirty minutes.
10 I meet him tomorrow at ten o'clock.
11 Has he come yet?

B Answer the following questions on **A** above.

1 In 1 how do we know that the train left before they got to the station?
2 How would substituting *walked* for *was walking* change the meaning of 2?
3 (a) Why is the verb in the second clause of 3 in a different tense from the verb in the first clause?
   (b) Would changing the form of the second verb to *will have finished making* change the meaning of the sentence?
   (c) Would changing the form of the first verb to *has finished* alter the meaning of the sentence?

4 Is the choice of tense in the second sentence of 4 crucial to the meaning of the sentence? Why?

5 Could the verbs in 5 be put into other tenses without seriously affecting the meaning of the sentence?

6 How important is the choice of tense in the first clause of 6 in indicating past habit?

7 Does the choice of tense in *when he comes* contribute to the meaning of the sentence in 7?

8 In 8 does the rail worker's choice of tense contribute significantly to the meaning of his utterance?

9 Could any other tense be used in 9 without changing the meaning of the sentence?

10 (a) What does the choice of tense in 10 tell us which we could not have deduced from the other elements in the sentence?

(b) What does it tell us which is also communicated by other elements in the sentence?

11 How important is the choice of tense to the meaning of sentence 11?

C The following incomplete statements refer to **A** above. Fill in the blanks.

1 In some utterances the choice of tense is crucial as the use of a different tense would ___ ___ ___ of the utterance.

2 In some utterances the choice of tense is not absolutely crucial as the ___ which it has been chosen to communicate is also communicated by ___ ___ in the utterance and/or by ___ ___ ___ ___.

3 In some utterances the tense does not contribute significantly to the ___ ___ ___ ___ as other elements of the ___ and the ___ make the ___ absolutely ___ . In such utterances the tense is chosen mainly for its ___ rather than for the ___ that it can convey and an error in the choice of tense would not necessarily ___ ___ ___ ___ ___ ___.

D Check your answers to **C** in the commentary, then complete the following table by putting each verb from **A** in the appropriate column. (The numbers at the head of the columns refer to statements 1–3 in **C** above.)

1	2	3
was walking (2)	got (1) had gone (1)	

E Write two examples of your own in which the choice of tense is crucial to the meaning of the utterance.

F Write two examples of your own in which the choice of tense reinforces the function of another element in the utterance.

G Write two examples of your own in which the verb tense is appropriate but is not crucial because other elements of the utterance or the situation communicate the same function.

H Complete the analysis of tense significance that follows this passage.

The old woman had been moved into the small room where the child had slept and the man with the red moustache had been shifted into what the nurse now called the convalescence room. In the middle room Jennifer lay with her eyes closed. They had apparently succeeded in removing the book as it was lying face down on the table.

Analysis

1 *had been moved* – the selection of the past perfect tense is crucial as it is the only indicator that the moving had been completed before the arrival of the writer.
2 *had slept* – the selection ...
3 ...

I Analyse the tense significance of the verbs in the dialogue below:

Mary: Here it is. It's been in this cupboard all the time we've been looking for it.
Simon: Good. I'll take it to the pub tonight. I'm meeting Arthur at nine; I'll give it to him then. I was going to buy him another one.
Mary: The phone's ringing.
Simon: I'll get it. Sam usually rings about this time.
Mary: It's stopped ringing. You didn't answer it quickly enough.

J What is the relevance of this unit to the teaching of the tenses of English?

17 Tense and aspect

A Sort these utterances into two categories based on the verbs. Describe your categories.

1 Fred went to London last week.
2 I was working for a cigarette company in May last year.
3 He's just having dinner.
4 I'll be at the meeting tomorrow.
5 Maggie goes fishing on Sundays.
6 I'll be lying on the beach at Torremolinos this time next week.
7 His house is being painted.
8 He visited India as a child.

B Account for these wrong utterances by learners of English:

1 *Q:* What did you do when the telephone rang?
   A: ✗ I wrote a letter.

2 *Q:* Cigarette?
   A: ✗ No thanks. I'm not smoking.

3 *Q:* What do you think of the government?
   A: ✗ I'm liking it very much.

4 *Q:* Where are you going?
   A: To town.
   Q: ✗ Will you go to the post office?

5 *Q:* What were you doing when the doorbell rang?
   A: ✗ I got up and opened the door.

6 *Q:* ✗ Where have you been last night?

7 *Q:* Who built that wall?
   A: ✗ The Romans had built it 2000 years ago.

C   In view of these typical and frequent errors, how do you think learners of English can be helped to understand the difference between tense and aspect?

18 Tense and function 2

A   Comment on these statements.

1 The simple past is always used for completed actions.
2 The most common use of the present continuous tense is to express the future.
3 The future tense is formed with *will* or *shall* + infinitive.
4 The past perfect tense is used to express the distant past.
5 Past and present tenses should not be used in the same sentence.

B   Provide a context for these sentences, and comment on the meanings of the verbs in each one:

1 He's always dropping cigarette ash on the carpet.
2 Paul Gascoigne scores for England at Wembley yesterday.
3 Becker serves to Edberg.
4 It leaves at 6.30.
5 We'll wait until they arrive.
6 Pure water boils at 100°C.
7 I never saw Caruso sing.
8 I've never been to a Bob Dylan concert.
9 Hemingway wrote *The Old Man and the Sea*.
10 Dickens wrote novels.
11 Wim Wenders directed *Paris Texas*.
12 Margaret Drabble has written a number of successful novels.
13 Gladstone would often take a hot water bottle filled with tea to bed.
14 I used to play football.

C   Comment on these errors.

1 ✗ John uses to get up early.
2 ✗ My brother lives in Kent for twenty-three years.
3 ✗ Did you finish your homework yet?
4 ✗ We've been in London yesterday.
5 ✗ Dinosaurs had died out millions of years ago.

D   Comment on the effectiveness of the following practice exercise for learners. What will they learn from it? What will they not learn?

Put the verbs in the following sentences into the correct tenses:

1 He (go) to bed late last night.
2 Willy (never be) to Paris.
3 John (drink) heavily but now he's a teetotaller.
4 The Blues (be born) in the Mississippi Delta.
5 Buddy Holly (give) a concert just before he died.
6 West Germany (win) the 1974 World cup.

E   Some uses of the simple present tense are exemplified in **B** above. Here is a more exhaustive list of uses. Match the uses in the left-hand column with the examples in the right-hand column, and put them in order to indicate teaching priorities. Give reasons for your decisions.

1 Expresses habits.   (a) Willy gets up at 7 every day.
2 Expresses action happening   (b) Sugar dissolves in warm water.
   at time of statement
3 Expresses general truths.   (c) The Carlisle bus arrives at noon.
4 Expresses predictable, regularly   (d) Joe smokes heavily.
   occurring events in the future.
5 Expresses routine.   (e) Mary speaks fluent Spanish.
6 Used in newspaper headlines and (f) Clinton calls for energy summit.
   photo captions to express recent
   past events.
7 Expresses facts about the present. (g) Rush passes to Hughes.
8 Expresses the future after certain   (h) We'll phone you as soon as we get home.
   time expressions.

19 Non-finite verb forms

A   Are the words in *italics* verbs, adjectives or nouns?

1 *Seeing* is *believing*.   6 He watched her *crossing* the room.
2 He's *waiting* for a taxi.   7 They've just done a *listening* exercise.
3 He's *playing* a *waiting* game.   8 The school is *being* redecorated.
4 Few people like *going* to the dentist's. 9 *Being* a doctor, he was able to help.
5 I hope you don't mind my *asking* … 10 She went upstairs *cursing* and *grumbling*.

B   **1** Replace the words in *italics* by a different word (not ending in *-ing*) which would fit in grammatically; the meaning is irrelevant.

eg Willy hates *dancing*.
    – Willy hates *cabbage*.

(a) The kettle is *boiling*.
(b) The film was *exciting*.
(c) I'm looking forward to *going to London*.
(d) We had pork, roast potatoes and *sprouting* broccoli for lunch yesterday.

(e) I'm not accustomed to *eating out*.
(f) Stop *talking*.

2 What have you learned from this process of substitution?

C What are the differences between the utterances in these pairs?

1 He stopped to look at the newspaper.
  He stopped looking at the newspaper.
2 Did you remember to lock the back door?
  Do you remember locking the back door?
3 Do you like dancing?
  Do you like to dance?
4 Do you like dancing?
  Would you like to dance?
5 She saw the burglar climb through the window.
  She saw the burglar climbing through the window.
6 I regret telling you that your road tax is overdue.
  I regret to tell you that your road tax is overdue.

D Comment on the errors in these utterances; put them right.

1 ✗ He has great difficulty to speak English.
2 ✗ I enjoyed to visit Cambridge yesterday.
3 ✗ He's used to go to bed late.
4 ✗ I'm looking forward to hear from you.
5 ✗ He tried starting his car but the battery was flat.
6 ✗ I've always been interested to take photographs of old buildings.
7 ✗ I don't feel like to go for a walk now.
8 ✗ I'm very pleased to seeing you.

20 Adverbs and adjectives

A Ask questions to elicit these answers (focus on the word(s) in *italics*).

1 It's *green*.
2 A *green* one.
3 The *green* one.
4 *Dangerously*.
5 *Quite frequently* – about once a week, in fact.
6 *Badly*.
7 Oh, he's a *good* dancer.
8 *Nearby*.

B Account for the errors:

1 ✗ Sally works hardly.
2 ✗ My friend speaks very well English.
3 ✗ How is the weather today?
4 ✗ Aberdeen is very far from London.
5 ✗ I've just been to visit my ill friend.
6 ✗ That's not a very usually colour for a car.
7 ✗ My sister is elder than I am.
8 ✗ He spoke to her friendlily.

C   Why do you think foreign learners may have problems with understanding or producing the words in *italics*?

1   The baby is rather *poorly* today.   4   Hold *tight*!
2   We have been visiting a *stately* home.   5   My brother isn't very *well*.
3   You should work *hard* and play *hard*.   6   He has an *elderly* uncle in Cardiff.

D   Which of the utterances 1–4 might be made:

(a) by an Eskimo in Zambia   1   It's too hot here.
(b) by an Eskimo in Britain   2   It's rather cold here.
(c) by a Zambian in Britain   3   It's too cold here.
(d) by a Zambian in Greenland?   4   It's quite warm here.

What are the factors influencing the choice of *quite*, *rather* and *too* to modify adjectives and adverbs?

21   Relative clauses

A   **1**   Identify the incorrect sentences and put them right.

(a) Peru, which is a very poor country, is known as the homeland of the Incas.
(b) The book, that you lent me last week, is on the shelf over there.
(c) He who laughs last laughs longest.
(d) Can you tell me more about the man you saw last night?
(e) Last week we went to see *Top Gun* which is a very good film but we couldn't stay till the end.
(f) Alexander Fleming, whose wife lived in Athens, died some years ago.
(g) Alexander Fleming was the doctor who discovered penicillin.
(h) *The Times*, that is known internationally as the voice of Britain, was not printed for several months during 1979.
(i) *Dallas* was an American TV series, which was very popular in Britain.
(j) *Dallas*, which was very popular in Britain, was an American TV series.
(k) When I was down in town I bumped into my cousin who told me the news.
(l) The man that did most for race relations in the United States was Martin Luther King.

2   Why is the comma such an important feature in these sentences?

B   In **A** you encountered two types of relative clause.

1   What is the function of a defining (restrictive) relative clause? Give an example from **A**.
2   What is the function of a non-defining (non-restrictive) relative clause? Give an example from **A**.
3   Are non-defining relative clauses common, quite common or fairly uncommon in spoken English? Why?

C   **1**   Why was it possible to omit a relative pronoun in the following utterances?

(a) The story you've just told me sounds plausible.
(b) I've told you before to be careful of people offering something for nothing.
(c) Everywhere you go you hear the same complaint.

(d) Nothing I have heard about him changes my opinion of him.

(e) An ammeter is an instrument used for measuring the strength of an electric current.

2 Why do you think some learners of English find it difficult to understand (and produce, when appropriate) utterances like these?

D Comment on these utterances in the light of exercises **A** and **C** above.

1 The girl in the red dress is from Canada.

2 They have just bought the old cottage on the hill above the village.

3 Please put out your cigarettes in the ashtray by the door.

E What might a learner of English find difficult about the relative clauses in the following utterances?

1 He failed his exams again, which naturally disappointed him.

2 She keeps on arriving late, which causes resentment among her colleagues.

F Account for these foreign learner errors.

1 ✗ The teacher lives opposite is a friend of mine.

2 ✗ The student which you spoke to yesterday is absent today.

3 ✗ The student who you spoke to him yesterday is absent today.

4 ✗ *Top Gun*? That's the film I got bored during.

5 ✗ She's not the little girl whom I once knew.

6 ✗ *Top Gun*, that I saw last week, is a boring film.

G What feature(s) do these utterances have in common?

1 It was Clara that you saw waiting at the corner.

2 It could have been Fred that rang you last night.

3 It was last Friday that I first felt ill.

4 Where was it that you spent the weekend?

5 What you see is what you get.

6 What you really believe is what is important.

22 Word order

A 1 What do these utterances have in common?

(a) What do you want to drink?

(b) Can you help me?

(c) Only by using a powerful microscope can you see the intricate cell-structure.

(d) Hardly had he arrived when the phone rang.

(e) You really should pay him back, shouldn't you?

(f) Pop goes the weasel (from a children's song).

(g) Here comes Willy at last!

(h) … and so say all of us!

(i) Under no circumstances must you contact the police.

(j) So be it.

(k) Willy hasn't finished yet and neither have I.

(l) Preparing to vault now is the world recorder-holder Sergei Bubka.

(m) Were you to ask me again, I might accept.

2 Account for the inversion of subject and verb in each of the examples above.

B   Explain the difference between these two types of inversion.

Type 1	*Type 2*
Nor do I.	There goes Charlie.
On no condition does he lend money.	'Hey-ho!' says Rowley.
Seldom do you hear such a delightful rendering of that aria.	Down the hill rolls the ball.

C   Explain the apparent inconsistency between the sentences in each pair.

(a) Here comes my friend v Here she comes.
(b) Up into the clear blue sky soared the bird v Up into the clear blue sky it soared.

D   Explain what is wrong with these utterances and produce at least one acceptable version of each one.

1   ✗ They go often to London.
2   ✗ My sister plays marvellously tennis.
3   ✗ I'm giving my daughter a pink cuddly new teddy for Christmas.
4   ✗ Where's your car? — I've lent John and his friends it.
5   ✗ Always I make that mistake!
6   ✗ That's a man's old coat. (But note the ambiguity in your corrected version!)
7   ✗ Nowhere am I going this evening. I'm staying at home.

Unit 3 **Vocabulary and vocabulary teaching**

1   Common myths and misconceptions about words

Write a response to each of the following statements. Indicate to what extent you agree with the statement and try to give examples to support your response.

1 It is not correct to use words with new meanings. *Gay* means lively and cheerful not homosexual.
2 The translation of a word should have exactly the same referent in the second language as the word does in the first language.
3 The translation of a word should convey the same attitudes towards the referent in the second language as the word does in the first language.
4 It is not correct to use words from another language when talking in English. So English skiers are wrong to talk to each other about the *piste* or the *après-ski* and English people living in Japan are wrong to refer to themselves as *gaijins*.
5 When we are speaking to somebody it is very important that we use the correct words with precision and that we never use words vaguely or carelessly (eg *Pass me that thing on the table please*).
6 Slang words should never be used in written English.
7 Words referring explicitly to toilet functions or to the sexual act should not be used in mixed company.
8 Words in a foreign language are best learned through definitions and translations.

2   Word fields and lexical relationships

A   Compare the meanings of *pick* in the following, then answer questions (a)–(f).

1 Pick that book up, will you?
2 How's Bill? – He's picking up.
3 He's been picked to play for England.
4 Why are you always picking quarrels?
5 He's the pick of a bad bunch.
6 I picked up a hitch hiker at Stumps Cross.
7 I'll pick you up at six.
8 He's always picking his nose.
9 I need to buy a new pick before we go climbing again.
10 He's a pickpocket.
11 Don't pick people to pieces all the time.
12 He got in by picking the lock.

(a) Put the above utterances into groups in which *pick* has a similar meaning.
(b) Is there a 'core meaning' of *pick*. If so what is it?
(c) If you were teaching vocabulary to an intermediate group and you were advised by your syllabus or textbook to teach the word *pick*, what teaching decisions would you make?

(d) A class were doing a comprehension exercise in which the sentence, *I'll pick you up at ten* occurred. A student asked, 'What does *pick* mean?' and was told by the teacher to look it up in a dictionary. Comment on the teacher's answer.

(e) What answer would you have given to the student's question in (d) above?

(f) What is wrong with the following method of teaching the word *port*?
Teacher: I noticed most of you got wrong the question about the ship not being able to get into port. Copy down the following definitions of *port*, learn them for homework and then write five sentences of your own using *port*.
port = a harbour; a gate or gateway; carriage, bearing; to carry a weapon diagonally across and close to the body; left-hand side of a ship; strong sweet, dark red wine of Portugal.

B **1** For each of the following pairs of utterances say in what ways the words in *italics* are similar and in what ways they are different.

(a) *A:* Did you know that William has become a *rebel*?
B: He hasn't. He's become a *freedom fighter*.

(b) *A:* I envy Alice. She's really *slim*.
B: Do you think so? I reckon she's *skinny*.

(c) *A:* He really is *mean*.
B: I wouldn't say that, I would say he was *thrifty*.

(d) *A:* He's *very fat*, isn't he?
B: He is. In fact I'd go as far as to say he's *obese*.

(e) *A:* He wears rather *feminine* clothes.
B: *Effeminate* would be more accurate.

2 What important vocabulary teaching points do the above pairs of sentences suggest to you?

C **1** Replace the words in *italics* in the following utterances with one of the following: *shoes, pen, meat, seat, picture.*

(a) Look at this *drawing*.
(b) I bought a new pair of *boots*.
(c) Lend me that *biro*, will you?
(d) I think we'll have *steak* for dinner.
(e) Put it on the *chair*, will you?
(f) That's a nice *photo*.
(g) That *sofa* is not very comfortable.
(h) I like your new *moccasins*.
(i) Is this your *fountain pen*?
(j) I'll have that *lamb* please.
(k) Did you do that *painting*?
(l) Sit in that *armchair* there.
(m) That blue *ballpoint* is mine.
(n) Let's sit down on this *bench*.

2 What is the effect of these substitutions on the meaning of the utterances?
3 What does this exercise suggest about the teaching of vocabulary to beginners and to advanced students?

D **1** What is wrong with the following utterances spoken by one friend to another? What do you think might have caused the speaker to use each of the utterances?

(a) ✗ I fractured a cup when I was washing up.
(b) ✗ He ejected the dog from the kitchen.
(c) ✗ Don't feign to me.
(d) ✗ Be careful. The bridge is feeble.
(e) ✗ Your ball pierced my window.

(f) ✗ I desire an ice-cream.

(g) ✗ Don't worry. I'll manufacture another paper aeroplane for your Willy.

(h) ✗ The buses were on strike so we had to march all the way to town.

2 What conclusions about the teaching of vocabulary does a consideration of the above errors lead you to?

E 1 What is missing from the following definitions?

mate = *friend*   guy = *man*
fag = *cigarette*   gear = *clothes*
bird = *girl*   It's gross = *I don't like it at all*
boss = *master or manager*

2 What errors could the learning of such definitions lead to? Give one example for each word.

3 What important points about the teaching of vocabulary does this exercise suggest to you?

F What ideas do the diagrams suggest for the teaching of vocabulary?

1

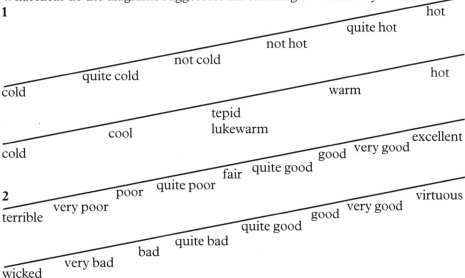

2

G Look at the use and misuse of the words in the following pairs of English words. Then come to conclusions about:

1 the difference between the words in each pair;

2 the criteria for deciding whether two words are interchangeable;

3 the use of synonyms (or near-synonyms) in the teaching of vocabulary.

reach/arrive

We reached home at ten.   ✗ He arrived out his hand.
We arrived home at ten.   He reached out his hand
I reached the French border at six.   ✗ We reached back at ten.
✗ I arrived the French border at six.   We arrived back at ten.
I reached that conclusion last night.   Can I reach you at the office?
I arrived at that conclusion last night.   ✗ Can I arrive you at the office?
He has just arrived.
✗ He has just reached.

brave/courageous
    That was a brave decision.
    That was a courageous decision.
    He's a brave man.
    He's a courageous man.
    He braved the storm.
✗ He couraged the storm.
    Making the decision to resign took great courage.
✗ Making the decision to resign took great bravery.
    Rescuing that boy from the fire was an act of great bravery.
    Rescuing that boy from the fire was an act of great courage.
    He didn't have the courage of his convictions.
✗ He didn't have the bravery of his convictions.
    Don't lose courage.
✗ Don't lose bravery.
    Hard luck, that was a brave try.
    Hard luck, that was a courageous try.

put up/accommodate
    Can you accommodate a party of ten students?
    Can you put up a party of ten students?
    Hey, Bill, can you put me up tonight?
    Hey, Bill, can you accommodate me tonight?

3   Factors in the teaching of vocabulary

A   1 Look at the following sentences and make conclusions about: (a) opposites in English, (b) the use of opposites in the teaching of vocabulary.

old/new
He's an old man.
He's an old friend.
I'll do it for old times' sake.
He's like a new man.
I think we'll try a new way to work today.

tall/short
That's a tall building.
That's a tall order.
I always seem to be short of breath.
I'm too short to join the police force.
This rope is too short.

work/leisure
He works in a leisurely way.
Mozart's works will live for ever.
He's at the works.
We need to educate people for leisure as well as work.

rough/smooth
He's very rough.
He got a rough deal.
It was a rough match.
This material is smooth.
He's a very smooth person.

rich/poor
Poor man, he's hurt.
That cake is too rich.
That's a poor idea.
He's rich in ideas.

light/dark
It was a light evening.
It was a light load.
It was a dark day for England.

2 For each of the above pairs decide whether you would ever teach them together and give the reasons for your decision.

B **1** The following were sentences used by different teachers to help them to exemplify the meaning of *amazed*. Look carefully at each example and then say why you think it is a good or a bad teaching example.

(a) I was amazed when he told me.
(b) I've never been so amazed in my life.
(c) He was absolutely amazed when he found out.
(d) I was really amazed when he told me he had failed the exam. The reason I was so surprised was that he had been getting very high marks all term. I was even more amazed when I found out that I had passed as all term I had been getting low marks.
(e) I was amazed by his death. I had never expected him to die so soon.

2 What conclusions have you come to about examples used to help teach the meanings of new words?

3 Write teaching examples for the following: *careful; clumsy; slippery; decide.*

C A teacher asked students to write a sentence using *swept* as it is used in the sentence *Mary swept the carpet every morning*.

Look at the sentences he got from the students. What do they tell you about:

1 the students' understanding of the meaning of *swept*?
2 this type of test question?

He swept it. I saw him.	She swept the carpets twice a week
Jane swept the carpet a lot.	Mary swept the carpet before she went to work.
Have you swept the carpet yet?	They didn't sweep the carpet very often.

D Deduce the meaning of the nonsense word(s) in *italics* in 1–3 and say what clues you found in the text to help you.

1 *A:* I found this *nibbit* in your pocket when I took your coat to be *slinned*.
   B: Oh yes, I put it in my pocket in case I was hungry at the football match.
   A: I prefer the ones with chocolate on myself.
   B: So do I. That's probably why I didn't eat it. When will my coat be ready?
   A: Tomorrow morning.
   B: I hope they get all the marks and stains out this time. I want to look smart at my interview.

2 *A:* Did you have to *ding* him so hard?
   B: He was very naughty.
   A: But you really hurt him.
   B: I know, I hurt my hand too. It was only his leg though.
   A: He'll soon get over it.

3 I was sitting in the garden reading when I felt a drop of rain. I didn't want the *glogget* to get wet so I got up, folded it up and went to put it in the garage with the other garden seats. When I saw the garage I was furious. It was so *unseddy*. I'd told the kids to put all their toys in the trunk to keep the garage *seddy* but now there were toys all over the garage floor.

What vocabulary teaching points does the above exercise suggest?

E **1** If the following words existed what do you think they would mean?

(a) *reget*   (f) *punkly*
(b) *cardback*   (g) *postthink*
(c) *excessage*   (h) *impossibliate*
(d) *sublunar*   (i) *disrecommend*
(e) *bidaily*   (j) *attendive*

2 What parts of speech (eg *noun*) would they be?
3 What vocabulary teaching points does this exercise suggest to you?
4 What advice would you give about teaching the following real words?
disinterested
ruthless
important
impose

F **1** Which sentences produced by the following substitution table are not acceptable or not normal in English?

1	2	3
It was	marvellous sensational amazing superlative superb incredible brilliant wonderful	to eat to watch to hear to drive

2 Can you make any valid generalizations as a result of doing this exercise?
3 What conclusions does the exercise lead you to regarding the teaching of the words in column 2?

G **1** Try to make as many acceptable sentences as possible from the following substitution table.

2 Discuss the differences in meaning between the words in column 2.

1	2	3	4
I've	bought purchased hired rented rented out sold borrowed acquired lent let loaned	a the my	house car money business pen tent television picture dog

H   Comment on the following vocabulary exercise.

> **Decide whether the words in column A can be used together with each of the numbered words. If two words *can* be used together put a tick in the relevant box. If they *cannot* put a cross.**
>
> | A | 1
believer | 2
supporter | 3
customer | 4
gardener | 5
student | 6
reader | 7
vegetarian |
> |---|---|---|---|---|---|---|---|
> | keen | | | | | | | |
> | fervent | | | | | | | |
> | enthusiastic | | | | | | | |
> | fanatical | | | | | | | |
> | interested | | | | | | | |
> | zealous | | | | | | | |

4   Phrasal and prepositional verbs

A   Group the verbs into two categories according to whether they are followed by adverbs or prepositions.

1   *Drink up* quickly.
2   He *switched* the light *off*.
3   Is this story true or did you *make it up*?
4   He has just *applied for* a new job.
5   We *called on* Willy yesterday.
6   In Germany, young men are *called up* at the age of 18.
7   Water *consists of* hydrogen and oxygen.
8   He was *looked upon* as a hero.

B   Comment on the verbs.

1   You'll have to *catch up on* what you've missed.
2   You mustn't *put up with* that!
3   Most western countries have *done away with* capital punishment.
4   You must *drop in on* us some time.

C   Turn these utterances into the passive. Read them aloud then identify and account for stress patterns in each.

1   Someone will have to speak to him firmly.
2   Someone will have to put this work aside.
3   Nobody can account for three of the crew.
4   They cleaned the house up after the party.
5   Someone has filled this form in.
6   Someone has laid up a lot of ships in the south-west of England.
7   Someone has shut down the steelworks.
8   Someone has worn this record out.

D   What are the meanings of the verbs in *italics*? Which can be deduced directly from the two parts of the verb?

1   Some learners *catch on* very quickly.
2   You're always *answering back!*
3   This milk has *gone off!*
4   Your new dress needs *to be let down.*
5   Our sponsors have *let* us *down.*
6   We'll have to *lay in* extra sugar supplies.
7   You shouldn't keep on *running* your friends *down.*
8   He was *put out* by your attitude.
9   *Stand up!*
10   He *ran away* from home when he was 6.
11   What time did you *knock off* last night?
12   My French needs *brushing up.*

E   Comment on the effectiveness of the following exercise.

Replace the verbs in *italics* with phrasal or prepositional verbs.

1 He had three teeth *extracted* yesterday.
2 He was *raised* in Scotland.
3 She *resembles* her mother.
4 The match has been *postponed* till next week.
5 You're always *disparaging* your brother.
6 That paragraph can be *omitted.*
7 His accent *betrayed* him as a Welshman.
8 Everyone feels the need to *escape* for a while.
9 Dinosaurs *became extinct* millions of years ago.
10 We must *reduce* our outgoings.

Unit 4 **Cohesion**

A   Look carefully at the words in *italics*, think about their function, then answer the
questions below.

   (a) Have you given *it* to *him* yet?
   (b) Are we seeing *them* again tonight?
   (c) Did you buy *it* from *him*?
   (d) Have *they* seen *it* before?
   (e) If I see *him* with *her* again I'll tell you.
   (f) Why did *she* get angry?
        He was very drunk.
   (g) *Hers* is beautiful.

   Questions
   1 Why is it not clear what the above sentences refer to?
   2 What is required to make the reference of the above sentences clear?
   3 Rewrite the sentences to make their reference clear.
   4 When would your sentences be more appropriate than the sentences above?
   5 When would the above sentences be more appropriate than your sentences?
   6 Are there any situations in which some of your sentences would actually be
      considered incorrect?
   7 *he, she, it, they, him, her* and *them* are personal pronouns. What do you think
      the main function of these pronouns is?
   8 *I, we* and *you* are also personal pronouns. Why can't you replace them with
      nouns in the above sentences?
      How are they different in function from the other personal pronouns?
   9 You have probably used *her* in your rewrite instead of *hers* (eg *Her house is
      beautiful*). What is the difference in function between *her* and *hers*?

B   **1** What has caused the breakdown in communication in the following
           conversations?

        (a) *A:* Are they going there again?
             B: Where?
        (b) *A:* I saw him then.
             B: When?
        (c) *A:* I'm doing those then.
             B: Which?
        (d) *A:* Did you buy that there?
             B: What?

     2 What do *there, then, those* and *that* have in common in the above examples?
     3 What words in the conversations could have caused a breakdown in
           communication and why didn't they?
     4 Rewrite *B*'s responses in each conversation so that she is indicating a different
           problem of communication.

45

C **1** Why is there very little danger of a breakdown in communication in the following sentences?

(a) I'll give you this instead.   (c) I'll see you here at six.
(b) Are these yours?   (d) Let's eat here now.

2 What is the main difference in function between:

(a) *this, these, here* and *now*   and   (b) *that, those, there* and *then* ?

D Look at the way *that* and *this* are used in the following utterances.

1 *A:* He broke her favourite vase.
   B: That was very valuable.
   A: That was very careless.

2 *A:* Don't worry. There'll be nobody in the house. We'll be on the road with the picture in ten minutes' time.
   B: I still don't like the idea.
   A: This is it now. Stop the car.
   B: This is crazy.

What is the main difference in function between the two instances of *that* in 1 and between the two instances of *this* in 2?

E **1** What is the potential difference in meaning between (a) and (b)?

(a) They were a different two books.
(b) They were two different books.

What is the difference between the grammatical function of *different* in (a) and *different* in (b)?

2 (a) Complete the following conversation:

   A: I need some other clothes.
   B: Not again? You bought some new shirts last week.
   A: No! I don't mean new clothes. I mean _____ clothes. I don't want to get these _____.

(b) What does the word *other* warn you to do in order to understand an utterance which contains it?

(c) Write a similar conversation in which *another* causes misunderstanding.

3 (a) What makes the following sentence ambiguous?

   We'll have to do more for them.

(b) Describe two situations in which the sentence would not be ambiguous. The sentence should not have the same meaning in both situations.

F **1** What do the words in *italics* have in common?

(a) Your cooker is not working properly.   – I know, I need a new *one*.
(b) Does anyone want to go to the pub?   – Yes, I *do*.
(c) Has the London train gone?   – I think *so*.
(d) My mother fusses and nags me all the time.   – Mine *does* too.
(e) I'll have a pint of bitter.   – I'll have the *same*.
(f) Will the game be postponed?   – I hope *not*.

(g) Don't bother washing the cups. We can use the old *ones*.

(h) I didn't get a paper today. Can I borrow *yours*?

(i) Can you give me a lift in your car? *Mine* has broken down.

2 The words in *italics* have very similar grammatical functions. However they can be divided into four distinct groups. Allocate each utterance to a group and say how each group is different from the others.

G **1** What do the following utterances in *italics* have in common?

(a) Mark bought a plant *and Lynn a basket of flowers*.

(b) Would you like to hear another song? *I know a lot*.

(c) What did you think of the lectures?   *–Two were quite good but two were awful*.

(d) I thought that one of the twins would get into the team *but I was surprised when both were selected*.

(e) *Has he gone?* – Yes, he has.

(f) Janet should have been informed *but I don't think she has been*.

(g) *Bill scored two and Fred one*.

(h) Has she been laughing? *– No, crying*.

(i) What should I have done? *– Phoned the police*.

2 Allocate each of the utterances in *italics* to one of two groups and describe the difference between group one and group two.

3 Use the examples above to help you to work out generalizations about what can be omitted in a second utterance or response.

H **1** Look at the following sentences and think about the differences in meaning between them.

(a) I like football *and* I like rugby.

(b) I like rugby *and* I like football.

(c) *As well as* football I like rugby.

(d) I like rugby *as well as* football.

(e) *In addition to* football I like rugby.

(f) I like rugby *in addition to* football.

(g) I like football. *Also* I like rugby.

(h) I like rugby. *Also* I like football.

(i) I like football. *In addition* I like rugby.

(j) I like rugby. *In addition* I like football.

2 Do the same exercise with the following sentences.

(k) It is an old car *but* it never lets me down.

(l) It is an old car. *However* it never lets me down.

(m) *Although* it is an old car it never lets me down.

(n) It never lets me down *but* it is an old car.

(o) It never lets me down. *However* it is an old car.

(p) It never lets me down *although* it is an old car.

3 Are there any differences in meaning between the different utterances in (a)–(j)? If so, say what they are.

4 The words in *italics* in (a)–(j) are examples of words and phrases which can be used to link two statements, ideas, etc together. They represent three different types of such words and phrases. *As well as, and* and *also* belong to different types. Distinguish between the three types and allocate each word or phrase in *italics* to one of your types.

5 What are the differences in meaning between the utterances in (k)–(p)?

6 Allocate each of the words in *italics* in (k)–(p) to one of the types you have established in **4** above.

I   **1** Look at the expressions in the box below and make up sentences exemplifying the use of each of them.

> instead   in that case   in any case   and also   similarly   because of this   in fact consequently   previously   despite this   then   for instance   however   so for this purpose   on the other hand   for example   furthermore   meanwhile therefore   thus   at the same time   on the contrary   with this in mind as a matter of fact   on account of this   as well as   likewise   finally   besides

2 Place each item in one of the types established in **H4** above.
3 Place each item in the appropriate category, as indicated below.

Exemplification	*Sequence*	*Reason*	*Result*	*Purpose*	*Comparison*
	first	for this reason	as a result		in the same way

Addition	*Contrast*	*Correction*	*Dismissal*	*Reinforcement*	*Time*
nevertheless	rather		anyhow	moreover	
even so	at least				

4 When you have filled in the columns examine the expressions in each column and then comment on the differences in use between the expressions.

J   Identify, correct and explain the errors in the following utterances.

1 ✗ The ship finally sank this morning. Meanwhile in Canada there has been an unprecedented heatwave.
2 ✗ It was a tremendously exciting match. Nevertheless I hope you enjoyed it.
3 ✗ I don't like musicals. Anyhow I'll come with you.
4 ✗ I don't like jazz. On the contrary I like folk music.
5 ✗ It was really cold in the factory. In that case they refused to work.

K   Complete the following sentences. Then make generalizations about the words you have used to fill in the blanks. When are they used and why?

1 We all kept quiet. That seemed the best _____.
2 Any ideas where I should stay in Hong Kong? I've never been to the _____ before.
3 What shall I do with all this equipment?
   Leave the st_____ here. We'll come back for it later.
4 I thought we were going to London today.
   I don't know where you got that _____ from.
5 Where shall I put this hairdryer?
   Put the t_____ away in that cupboard.
6 Bill's been stealing apples again. I'll have to teach that _____ a lesson.
7 Mrs Biggins has been spreading rumours about you again. That _____ is a damn nuisance.
8 She's feeding her dog. That cr_____ eats more food than I do.

L 1 This Unit has focused on cohesion (ie the ways in which we indicate connections between utterances). Read the following passage in order to gain a general understanding of it. Then read it again and identify all the markers of cohesion (eg *She* in sentence 4).

Dial M for Murder by Mother

OUR TELEPHONE bill is £325. I do not find this amusing. Treasure apparently does. She finds the whole thing hugely entertaining. She ignores repeated requests and reasonable arguments to limit usage, and when I finally approach, maddened, screaming hoarsely, 'Get off the phone!' she will smirk in a relaxed way into its mouthpiece.

'She wants me to get off the phone,' she drawls, cool as anything, moving it a tiny bit away from her ear and enabling her chum to hear the silly mother roaring in the background.

She is dicing with death. The dog knows. It is hiding under the kitchen table, looking crumpled, but Treasure doesn't care. She will risk anything to use the phone. Returning home from even the briefest excursion, she will dart to it, grab it and cradle it on her knee. 'Who can I phone?' she asks, staring wildly into the air. She strokes its little plastic body. 'I'll phone Lizzie,' she cries. 'No you

won't. It isn't six yet.'

'I must. I've got to.' Treasure is desperate for her next fix. Her addiction has worsened over the past six months. She waits till six. She is on hot coals. She cannot rest, work or eat. She stalks the house, watching the clock, waiting, hoping someone will ring and break her vigil. At six she clamps herself to the telephone, talking and laughing fiercely. I could hear every top-volume word from the bottom of the garden but Treasure is determined I shall not listen.

'Shut the door,' she roars bossily as I leave the room. I refuse. I am carrying a mountain of dirty cups, plates, banana and orange skins, and chewed yoghurt pots which she and the dog have discarded. I haven't a free hand.

I don't really want the door shut anyway. Once it's shut, the dog cannot get in or out freely and starts to bark and scratch, and when Treasure is on the phone she is unable to move and attend to the dog's needs. It can scratch

its claws off and bark itself dumb, and Treasure will not move a muscle. I am forced to return on such occasions and let it out myself.

'Why didn't you open the door?' I snap. 'I didn't hear,' says Treasure, looking hurt. 'Really I didn't.'

But she can hear the telephone, even on the quietest ring and hidden under my double duvet. Someone phones at 10pm, Treasure's supposed bedtime. 'She's asleep,' I growl. But she has heard its tiny muffled ring. She crawls exhausted from her bed.

'Who was it?' she croaks. She cannot sleep without this knowledge. She cannot sleep with it. She will lie awake wondering what vital snippet she has missed and planning tomorrow's return call. And there's the rub. Put them off today and the little toads will only ring back tomorrow. The return calls mount up, a cumulative effect. I know that tomorrow will also be a hell of ringing, shrieking and arguing, and may end in

violence. Grandma, among others, will be coming out in spots down in Hove, trying to get through.

I have wrenched the phone from its socket, smacked it from her hand, fisticuffs have ensued and the solution seems no nearer. 'Get Treasure her own phone,' say the Liberals. 'Tell her that this is not acceptable,' say the Cleverdicks, but at last Mrs Perez has come up with a possible answer: what about Treasure's own phone but for incoming calls only? Then they can all phone her on that and at least my line will be clear. All I'll have to worry about is when, behind her closed bedroom door, glued to her own telephone, will Treasure ever do her homework and go to sleep?

'She's only copying you,' says Mrs Perez cruelly. 'What do you do when you're upset? You run to the phone and tell everyone.' My fault again. Now we know who is responsible for Britain's economic crisis. Mr Lamont's mother.

from the *Guardian*, 2 March 1993

2 Set comprehension questions which would help learners to understand the functions of the examples you have identified.

M What are the teaching implications of the discoveries you have made as a result of doing the exercises in this Unit?

Unit 5   **Coherence**

A   Look carefully at the following dialogues.

Analyse each utterance as in the following example.

	Type	*Purpose*
1 *A:*	interrogative	offer
B:	declarative	declining offer

1 *A:* Would you like a cigarette?
  B: No thanks.
  A: It's OK. I've got plenty more.
  B: I don't smoke.

2 *A:* It's raining, isn't it?
  B: Yes, it is.
  A: I'd better go and get my raincoat then.
  B: Could you get mine as well please?

3 *A:* It's two o'clock.
  B: Don't worry. I'm nearly ready.
  A: It'll take us at least fifteen minutes to get there.
  B: Do you ever stop worrying?

B   **1**   Describe situations in which the following exchanges would make sense.

(a) *A:* It's nearly seven
    B: Yes, I know. I'm just going to ring him now.

(b) *A:* The grass needs cutting.
    B: It's nearly ten o'clock.
    A: He'll wait.
    B: Like last week and the week before.
    A: The Robinsons are coming tomorrow.
    B: It's starting to rain now anyway.

(c) *A:* Shall we stop for a while?
    B: If you want.
    A: The Cow's quite good, isn't it?
    B: If you say so.
    A: We met your friend Jane last time, didn't we?
    B: My mother will be worried.

(d) *A:* Hello.
    B: Bob?
    A: I'm not coming tonight.
    B: He's already gone.
    A: Already?
    B: Try Ted's.

2 Analyse each utterance in each of the above dialogues in the same way as the following example.

		Type	Purpose
(a)	*A:*	declarative	getting somebody to do something
	B:	declarative	indicating acceptance of suggestion in *A*

3 What implications for teaching does your analysis of the exchanges in **A** and **B** reveal?

C The imperative sentence, *Do it now* can be interpreted in different ways according to the situation. It could be interpreted as any one of: command, advice, appeal, instruction or warning.

1 Match each of the following mini-dialogues with one of the five functions above.

(a) *A:* What do you think?
B: Do it now. Then it'll be dry when we come back.

(b) *A:* Do it now. There's somebody coming.

(c) *A:* Do it now.
B: Yes, sir.

(d) *A:* Do it now. Please, I want to go home.

(e) *A:* You need to turn it over very quickly. Do it now.

2 List the set of conditions which you think must prevail for the sentence to be interpreted as each of the five speech acts listed above.
eg *Command*
(a) *A* in authority over *B*
(b) *B* accepts authority of *A*
(c) *A* wants *B* to do something

3 How can such a listing of conditions help the teacher?

4 Write mini-dialogues for each of the following pictures. Then label each dialogue with one of the five functions.

(a)   (b)   BRAVO (c)

D Read the following paragraph.

The suggestion that all industries should be nationalized is ridiculous. Can you imagine the cost and the chaos? Look what happened to the railways. And the steel industry. No. Instead let us encourage private enterprise. Only then will we have initiative and thus prosperity.

Now answer the following questions.

1 What speech act (see Q4) does the question, *Can you imagine … perform?*
2 What speech act is performed by, *Look what happened to the railways?*
3 What two propositions does *instead* connect?
4 What does *then* refer to in the last sentence?
5 What is the function of *thus* in the last sentence?
6 The following analysis of the strategic structure of the above paragraph is wrong. Correct it.
    (a) Statement (sentence 1)   (d) Refutation
    (b) Question   (e) Conclusion
    (c) Exemplification   (f) Qualification of conclusion.

E Read the following.

We have a problem. Yesterday I was told that we couldn't have any more books this year as our budget has been spent. That means of course no tapes for the winter term. However I think I've got an answer. If your brother can lend us the tapes from his school we can lend him that spare set of 'Mullens' for the term.

Now answer the following questions.

1 What is the problem? How do you know?
2 What does *that* refer to in sentence 3?
3 What two propositions does *however* (in sentence 4) connect?
4 Does the *we* include or exclude the addressee? How do you know?
5 What does *Mullens* refer to? How do you know?
6 What implications for teaching have you discovered from doing 1–5 above?

F Identify and analyse the errors in the following extract from a student's work.

The most significant influence is the purchasing power of consumers. Nowadays, people tend to use central heaters rather than coal. Furthermore, the level of income altered the life style of the consumers. They prefer to use modern electrical appliances such as the electric kettle.

Another factor is the change in transportation. The increase in petrol led to the increase in transport especially the electrification of railway and motor vehicles. However, other types of industries increased from 15,210 million therms to 18,455 million therms as a result of the decrease in the iron and steel industry.

G   Cohesion and coherence are obviously both concerned with ways of connecting utterances together. It is not easy to actually define the difference between the two as there is considerable overlap between them. Try to complete the following definitions.

Cohesion involves indicating the conn———— between consec———— or rel———— utterances. If a text is cohesive you can see by loo———— at the text how one utterance is rel———— to a prev———— or subseq———— utterance.

Coherence is the lin———— together of conse———— or rel———— utterances according to the func———— of the utterances. Thus an invitation followed by an acc———— would be coh———— whereas an invitation followed by an anecdote would probably not be coh————.

Look at the following examples.

1 Mr Burns is often late. Yesterday I answered the phone.
2 *A:* Which platform does the London train go from?
   B: London? My daughter lives in London. She married a banker there last year.

Example 1 could be coh———— because it could consist of a generalization followed by an example and a consequence. But it is not coh———— because there is no ind———— ———— conn———— between the two utterances.

Example 2 is coh———— because the two utterances are connected by the repetition of *London*. But it is not coh———— because there is no apparent connection between the function of the question and the function of the reply.

Unit 6 Errors

1 Some myths and misconceptions about errors

Write a response to each of the following statements indicating to what extent you agree with it. Try to give examples to justify your views.

1 A good language learner makes very few mistakes when using the new language.
2 If learners make mistakes when speaking it is a result of errors in their learning.
3 Mistakes are caused by learners being lazy and failing to memorize what they are taught.
4 It is important that learners do not get away with making errors. They should be made to correct every error they make.
5 If errors go uncorrected they become habitual and impossible to eradicate.
6 Most errors are caused by interference from the first language. Such errors can be prevented by the teacher contrasting the two languages.

2 Learners' errors

A 1 Correct the errors in the following sentences and say what you think might have caused each of the errors.

(a) ✗ My father is a *fisher*.
(b) ✗ I *am seeing* a lion in that cage.
(c) ✗ He *like* football.
(d) ✗ He *leaves* in a large house.
(e) ✗ When I *will go* there tomorrow I will visit Mary.
(f) ✗ She's beautiful, *isn't it*?
(g) ✗ He *has gone* there this morning.
(h) ✗ Will you *borrow* me your car?
(i) ✗ He *has robbed* all my money.
(j) ✗ I rang up *so I booked* the tickets.
(k) ✗ He *had gone* to London yesterday at two.
(l) ✗ He *was wounded* in the car crash.
(m) ✗ If *he asked* I would have helped him.
(n) ✗ Suddenly *there came a friend* to me.
(o) ✗ We were *to* noisy.
(p) ✗ *This couldn't care us a* rap.
(q) ✗ I'm going to the lake *for swimming*.
(r) ✗ *My mother she is* very old.
(s) ✗ Mary doesn't like Jim. *He* says he is selfish.
(t) ✗ I have stopped *to play* football because of my injury.

2 Make a list of causes of learner errors from an analysis of the errors above.

B Look at the transcript below of part of a conversation between two elementary learners and then:

1 List all the errors.
2 Correct the errors.
3 Select the main types of errors and say what might have caused the students to make these errors.
4 (a) Imagine you are a teacher listening to this conversation. Would you correct the learners? Give reasons.
(b) If you answered 'Yes' to question (a), state *which* errors you would correct and *when* you would correct them.

A: I will be football player when I will be back to my home.
B: I will be professor in school.
A: What for?
B: I will enjoy. It will be nice to be teach.
A: No, it is bore. Football will be interest. It will be rich.
B: Professor will be rich too.
A: No, not true. Football player will be very much rich.
B: In my country football player not be rich, not give the money.
A: In my country he will be give lot of money.

C Compare the following extracts from an elementary learner's workbook. The second extract was written two weeks after the first.

> *Yesterday I bought book from shop. It cost £2. I read last night.*
>
> *Last week I buyed a new shirt from a shop in Cambridge. It cost me £10. I weared it at the party.*

1 What are the main differences between the two extracts?
2 What do you think might have been responsible for the differences?

D What can you discover about the learner's problems from reading this extract from his work?

> *My brother lives in a village but work in a town. Usually he cycles to his work however sometimes he goes by bus. His work is very tiring nevertheless he plays football and train when he comes home.*

E 1 List and correct all the errors in this extract from a learner's composition. Underline all the errors that you think should be given remedial attention by the teacher.

> *A TERRIBLE DREAM*
> *One day in September, the weather was fine and I worked the whole day. I was very tired, I went to my bed and fell asleep. Suddenly there came a friend to me and asked me to go with him. That friend died 5 years before, so it was very strange to meet him. I went with my friend. We walked in a very dark hall and when there were stairs, we went upstairs. We went to a room to*

see a garden of flowers. But there were no flowers, there was only a very strange man, his shin was very strange. He had a scarp in his face, he was very ugly. He beckoned me to come near. I was afraid, but I had to go near because in my back there were two men holding a gun. I went near, the man had a knife in his hand.

He wanted to murder me because his friend died two weeks before from an accident with my father. I said I could manage it, so he got a lot of money. He would gave me three hours to do everything in order. My friend and I were tied on a chair. We made up a story.

When the man came back, we should run away as fast as we could to the nearest police station.

After a time they came back, they had talked to my father. He wouldn't give any money they said, so they had to kill me. He took his knife to my heart. He want to come near with his knife. I shouted very hard and my mother came to my room. She asked what there was happened I said that it was only a bad dream.

2 Divide the errors you have identified into broad categories.

F List and correct all the errors in this transcript of an advanced learner telling the story of a cartoon. Which of the errors do you think might impede communication?

In a little local village Mr and Mrs Robinson wanted to watch the weekend film, when Mr Robinson switched on television he saw it didn't seem to work, so he went outside to discover that the television aerial had been broken down. That's why he tried to fix the ladder, to get a ladder and get on to the roof to fix it ... The ladder fell away, so he had to shout for help. His wife came outside and saw what was happening so she immediately called the fire brigade. When they arrived they succeeded in getting Mr Robinson safely on earth again. The three of them, Mr and Mrs Robinson and the man ... were standing there. Then at home Mrs Robinson made a hot cup of tea, and they were sitting together there, trying to watch TV to see a part of the weekend film but when they switched on television, the only thing they saw was 'The End.'

G 1 List and correct all the errors in this extract from a student's story.

He has been taken to hospital to see his friend. He came back an hour later but then went home. He said he had only been in hospital for ten minutes because the bus broke down and he must walk. He arrived at the hospital after closing time but because he has lonely the nurse granted him permission to see his friend shortly. If he told me he was going to the hospital I could give him a lift. Then he would have stayed with his friend a lot longer.

2 Give one example from the extract of each of these types of error:

(a) A lexical confusion which could impede communication.

(b) An expression which is too formal for the situation.

(c) An adverbial confusion which in another context could impede communication.

(d) A prepositional phrase confusion which in another context could impede communication.

(e) A tense error which could cause a time reference confusion.

H **1** Tabulate your opinion about each of the following statements.

Statement	Agree	Disagree	Not sure
(a) The teacher should always correct learners' errors as soon as they make them.			
(b) Making errors can be useful for learners.			
(c) The teacher should relate decisions about correction to the objectives of the lesson.			
(d) The teacher should control activities so that they help the learners to avoid making errors.			
(e) When giving back written work it is better to focus on a few similar errors than to correct every one.			

2 Rewrite any of the statements you disagree with so that the new version reflects your views.

3 Explain why you agree with each of the other statements.

◑ Commentary

THE FOLLOWING COMMENTARIES suggest possible answers to most of the questions in the exercises. In many cases various other answers would be acceptable but are not included because of considerations of space. A few of the questions are so open-ended and specific to the individual reader's own experience that it has been decided not to provide commentary for them.

Unit 1 Myths and misconceptions

1 The English language

A Encouraging students to read only the classics of English literature does not necessarily help them to speak English well. Some reasons for this are:

- The classics were written a long time ago and therefore exemplify English expressions which are no longer current (eg third extract)

- Many of the classics include dialogue which exemplifies regional dialects very different from the standard English dialect we teach in the classroom (eg first extract).

- The syntax and style of the written English of the classics is very different from that of the spoken English of today (eg second extract).

- There is no such thing as the *best English*. An utterance in English is good if it succeeds in communicating the speaker's or writer's meaning and intention and if it is appropriate to the situation in which it is used. Reading only the classics can give learners the false impression that they should always try to use literary English.

- It is important that learners of English are given practice in reading the different types of modern written English which they are likely to come across outside the classroom.

B 1 English in its present form is not ancient at all and it is certainly not pure. It is the current stage in a process of evolution which has been influenced by contact with many other languages (eg Anglo-Saxon, Latin, Greek, French, Dutch) and with many regional varieties of English (eg Australian English, Indian English and American English). Change is inevitable in a language and borrowings and coinings are an important part of this change.

Such emotive words as *great, corruption, vulgar* and *pure* are not appropriate in a description of language development and there is not much point in fighting *against* what has already happened to a language.

2 The writer is engaging in a futile piece of prescription, saying that the grammar book and the dictionary have more authority than the language user. What the writer says is unacceptable is in fact common usage.

As teachers we should concern ourselves with what is said, not what we think ought to be said.

3 This statement is demonstrably untrue (eg *Have you found some?*; *I'll deal with any questions at the end*). However at an early stage of language learning it might be a useful over-simplification to make to certain learners, providing that the truth is subsequently revealed.

4 This is demonstrably untrue (eg *to pity*, *to fear* and *to expect* are verbs but not doing words; *running* – as in *running is good for you* – is a doing word but functions as a noun not a verb). At no stage of learning is this a useful over-simplification as it misleads learners without helping them to use the language.

5 This statement, too, is also neither true nor useful. The subjects of many sentences are neither people nor things (eg *What she says makes sense*) and very often the subject does not do any action (eg *He is hoping to go to university*).

6 Tense is not the same as time reference. The past tenses are often used with past time reference but not always (eg *I was thinking of going to the match tomorrow*; *I wondered if you would allow us to miss the meeting*; *If he came it would be too late*).

7 This statement is confusing as it is obvious that you can count money. It would be more accurate to say that uncountable nouns cannot be preceded by a number (eg ✗ *two rices*; ✗ *four monies*). NB ✗ = incorrect utterance.

8 *Will* is used in such clauses with the function of expressing *willingness* (eg *Let me know when he will do it*). The statement is designed to prevent such errors as, ✗ *I will phone you when he will arrive*, and can be a fairly useful over-simplification if it is made less absolute (ie *not often* instead of *never*).

9 Such people need to be able to use the variety appropriate to the situation in which they are communicating (eg Nigerian English in informal situations in Nigeria but Standard English at international conferences).

10 They are perfectly acceptable substitutes in very informal communication between social peers (eg friends, colleagues, members of the same team or group).

11 Formal jargon used in informal communication can be very annoying. However it can help to achieve economy and precision in formal discourse (eg *dwelling* can cover house, flat, bungalow, hut, caravan, etc).

12 There is a common misconception that foreigners talk very quickly because what you do not understand appears to be said more quickly than what you do understand. The learner finds the teacher easier to understand than a stranger because he or she has got used to the teacher's accent and speech mannerisms and because the teacher makes a deliberate attempt to be clearly understood.

It is important that learners are exposed to many different voices and that they participate in authentic conversation as well as practice drills in the classroom. It is especially important that the teacher does not always talk to learners in an artificially slow and precise way, as what is gained in immediate convenience will not compensate for future frustration.

13 Such a teacher will inevitably produce learners who stand out as being out of touch with current usage, who get frustrated by the discrepancy between what they are taught and what English speakers actually do, and who are inhibited by the constant demand for correctness.

Such a teacher also fails to appreciate the difference between spoken and written English and the fact that what is considered to be correct depends on the situation in which the language is being used. He also makes the arrogant mistake that a lot of experience automatically equals a lot of wisdom.

14 There is no such thing as *incorrect English*. There are many regional varieties of English. Each one is different from the others but all are equally correct. Standard English is the variety of English normally taught to foreign learners as this is the variety normally used by educated users of English regardless of their regional origins. The accent (ie way of pronouncing) normally taught to foreign learners is RP (Received Pronunciation). This accent is the one taught because it was the first one analysed and described and because many of the early English teachers and material designers spoke an approximation of it. However the users of this accent (often called BBC or Oxford English) are in the minority and can be defined as educated speakers of English whose accent is entirely uninfluenced by the accent of their region of origin. As most learners of English will eventually be exposed to many different English accents it is a good thing if some of their teachers are not RP speakers.

15 A good English speaker uses the type of English most suited to the situation. In some informal conversations slang is very suitable (eg an argument between friends in a pub about a football match).

2 Learning English

A A language cannot be said to be stupid because it is not completely regular and is not completely controlled by rules. No living language is completely regular and rule-bound because living languages are organic and are constantly being changed by their users.

- It is common for learners of a language to think that their own language is logical and regular and that the one they are learning is stupidly irregular. This is usually because they very seldom examine their own language whereas they are frequently called upon to examine the language they are learning. They also find their own language easy to use and assume that this is because it is logical and regular.

- English has been influenced by many other languages (eg Anglo-Saxon, Latin, Greek, French) and it contains many apparent illogicalities. However, like all languages, it operates as a system of generalizations, not as a system of absolute rules. Thus it is possible to make generalizations about the formation of the simple past tense in English (see 3) but it is easy to think of exceptions. The important thing to remember is that when formulating generalizations about a language you should describe what people using the language actually do and not prescribe what they should do.

- No language follows a set of fixed rules. Languages evolve and then grammarians attempt to describe them sometimes unfortunately making it seem that the patterns and regularities underlying the language are rules to be obeyed by the users of the language.

- The speaker in 5 seems to be following no rules. But in fact she is being more systematic and consistent than at first it appears.

- There are *some* patterns in English that *are* extremely regular and could be taught as rules. The doubling of the consonant after short vowel sounds is one (see 1), as is the agreement in person between the statement and the tag in English question tags (see 2).

B The pupil has imitated the form of a structure used by the teacher. In each case the pupil has made an error because the form he has used has not been appropriate. In 1 he uses the present continuous tense but this is inappropriate when referring to an ailment or illness; in 2 he uses the present perfect inappropriately to refer to a specific point of time in the past; and in 3 he uses 'will' to refer to the future in a time clause in which the appropriate verb form is the simple present tense.

It is obvious from the evidence that learning a language purely through imitation of correct forms can lead to the making of errors even when the forms are imitated correctly. It is important to be able to reproduce the correct forms of English structures but it is also very important to know when to use them and when not to use them. This cannot be learned from the imitation of forms.

C 1 The writer breaks all the rules that he imposes on his learners and thus demonstrates the frequent contradiction between actual usage and prescriptive rules. He uses *will* with *I*, he uses *who* instead of *whom* (*the pupils who I teach*), he splits an infinitive (*to always speak*) and he ends his sentence with the preposition *with*.

All the rules that he insists on (but breaks) refer to generalizations that used to be valid when describing the written English of the highly educated. None of them is valid today. They certainly do not describe what 'correct' speakers of English do today and therefore learners of the language do not need to follow them.

2 This statement illustrates the dangers of learning lists of uncommon words and then trying to show off the new words. The writer has learned the forms of many words that are not commonly used in English and has retained an approximate knowledge of their meaning. However he has not learned the restrictions on their use and his accumulation of inappropriate and unusual words will inevitably result in a ridiculous failure to communicate. New words are best learned in context and not from lists. It is not a good idea for learners of English to try to learn and use every *long* or unusual word they come across.

D 1 Grammar books and dictionaries are important sources of information about a language. They can teach someone about a language but they cannot teach anyone to use a language as they cannot expose the learner to language in real use and they do not provide any opportunities for practice or production.

2 A language can be learned in this way if the learner is strongly motivated and if the texts read and listened to are sufficiently comprehensible. However a teacher can help to make the process much more economical and effective by providing suitably comprehensible material, by focusing attention on salient features of the language and by providing help, encouragement and feedback.

3 Repetition of correct forms can help the learner to achieve automatic mastery of the formal elements of some structures (eg word order, verb endings, subject–verb agreement) but this does not help the learner to know why and when to use the structures.

4 There is much more to speaking a language than knowing its grammar (eg using structures, phrases and vocabulary appropriate to the purpose and context of the communication). Also declarative knowledge (knowing about) is not the same as procedural knowledge (knowing how). Furthermore, the grammar of spoken English is very different from the written grammar normally taught in textbooks.

5 This does not seem to be true for most learners. They seem to need training in using these skills in the foreign language regardless of their level of linguistic competence.

6 Listening and reading have many sub-skills (eg visualization, prediction, inferencing) in common but differ markedly in how these skills are used (eg reading usually allows a lot more time and thought than listening). In order to become an efficient listener you need a lot of experience of listening.

7 The grammar of spoken English is very different from the grammar of written English. Learners who speak as though they are writing sound very stilted and formal and often annoy the people they are trying to communicate with (eg compare, 'I've been thinking about it, maybe I'll – yeah maybe next Tuesday' with 'I have been giving the matter thought and have decided that maybe I will do it next Tuesday.')

8 This is a common mistake in textbooks and leads to the sort of stilted learner English referred to in 7 above. In order to develop the ability to use spoken English effectively you need experience of spoken English.

9 Some pronunciation 'errors' are amenable to correction (eg those consonants such as <u>thin</u> which are produced near the front of the mouth and are therefore 'observable') but most other 'errors' are resistant to constant correction (especially errors involving vowel sounds). Such a punitive approach to pronunciation errors can deflate and demotivate learners and actually prevent them from developing a pronunciation which, while not of native speaker standard, can achieve the only realistic target of international intelligibility.

10 Language learning needs the sort of constructive noise made by learners interacting with the teacher and with each other. Without it they will not gain the natural input they need nor the vital experience of using the language for oral communication.

3   Terminology

A 1 particular way; represented; writing; speech.
roles; plays; purpose; express.
form; function; form; function.
2 form; written; spoken; period; time; past; present; future; utterance.
3 full; contracted.
4 formal; official; serious; superiors; strangers; informal; relaxed; casual; know; well.
5 correct; acceptable; situations; people.
6 cotext; words; before; after; context; situation/setting.

B 1 (b)   2 (d)   3 (f)   4 (c)   5 (e)   6 (a)   7 (g)   8 (h)

Unit 2 Common areas of difficulty

1 Basic grammatical terms

A

1 noun	9 adverb	17 conjunction
2 noun	10 noun or intransitive verb	18 noun
3 verb (intransitive)	11 pronoun	19 noun
4 adjective	12 adjective	20 intransitive verb
5 conjunction	13 transitive verb	21 conjunction
6 preposition	14 adjective	22 preposition or adverb
7 pronoun (possessive)	15 adverb	23 noun
8 verb (intransitive)	16 intransitive verb	24 pronoun

B 1 One likely categorization is:

Concrete nouns	*Abstract nouns*	*Proper nouns*
elephant	delay	Poland
car	hope	Diana
mirror	truth	September
marmalade	humour	
oak	excitement	
radio		
telegraph pole		

2

Countable nouns		*Uncountable nouns*	
raisin	book	sugar	rice
nut	teaspoon	butter	spaghetti
cake	shop	milk	water
pound	pot	honey	
carton			

C Utterances containing transitive verbs: 1, 2, 4, 6, 7, 10.

Utterances containing intransitive verbs: 3, 5, 8, 9.

D 1 a restaurant; quite a while; the only one in town; a few questions; some rather lazy replies; something safe; a beef casserole; red meat; her; a cheese salad; the last portion; the cheese salad; a tip.

2 took; asked; gave; brought; asked; offered; didn't leave.
Two examples will suffice to explain the relationships involved:
(a) *It took me quite a while to …*
The verb *took* has a direct object (*quite a while*) and an indirect object (*me*) which could be moved and preceded by *for*.
(b) *She gave me some rather hazy replies …*
the verb *gave* has a direct object (*some rather hazy replies*) and an indirect object (*me*) which could be moved and preceded by *to*.

3 Other common verbs in this category include: *lend, get, promise, buy*, etc. Such verbs are sometimes called **ditransitive** verbs. Most transitive verbs, however, need only one object as there is no additional relationship involved, eg *I looked for a restaurant, I don't eat red meat.*

E 1 *because* (a conjunction) is wrongly used as a preposition.
  2 Subject pronoun *she* is wrongly used where object pronoun *her* is required.
  3 *quickly* (an adverb) is wrongly used as an adjective.
  4 *during* (a preposition) is wrongly used as a conjunction.
  5 *avoid* (a transitive verb) is wrongly used intransitively.
  6 *slow* (an adjective) is wrongly used as an adverb.
  7 *gives* (3rd person singular form of verb) is wrongly used after 3rd person plural pronoun *they*.
  8 *listen* is wrongly used with a direct object, perhaps by analogy with *hear*. (A preposition – *to* – is needed to make the utterance correct.)

F Because the structure words *he, his, and, out, a, they, until, a, to, them* are all recognizable and give an acceptable framework to the nonsense words, and because some of the nonsense words are marked by their endings as verbs ('crattl*ed*', 'strenter*ed*', 'veen*ed*') or adverbs ('folic*ly*'), or simply sound right in context.

G Depending on the dictionary, they may or may not appear as headwords. In any case none of them is the obvious form for a dictionary to list. A verb is normally listed under its infinitive, and a noun in its singular form.

H 1 (a) give, show
  (b) several possibilities, eg imperfections, paradoxes, contradictions, confusion
  (c) stuff
  (d) thought, could, were, built, grown, become
  (e) Midnight
  (f) many examples, eg act, learn, think
  (g) many examples, eg if, but, as if
  (h) correctly, intellectually, really, very

  2 This discussion might go in many different directions. Holt's point is that children use language to help them make sense of the world, but it sometimes only adds to the confusion. Younger children are certainly likely to find relatively **abstract** notions such as 'conjunction' or 'preposition' more difficult to handle than 'noun' or 'adjective'. There are many different possible ways of introducing word classes to children (eg 'a noun is a naming word', 'a verb is a doing word', etc – this often involves oversimplification or distortion), and you may be able to recall your own struggles with these terms during early school-days. Second or foreign language teachers may face problems with word classes if their learners never mastered them in their mother tongue. However, most learners will at least have acquired the basic means of describing the world around them by the time they start to learn a second or foreign language.

2 Forms and functions

A All the utterances express habitual or routine actions, signalled in different ways:

1 by the present simple verb
2 by the adjective and noun
3 by the *used to* structure (discontinued habit)
4 by the phrase *in the habit of*
5 by the association of *always* with the verb in the present continuous form.

B All the utterances contain verbs in the present continuous form, expressing something different each time:

1 an *ongoing* process (over a long undefined period)
2 something happening now (for a short period)
3 an expression of future intention; the meaning here depends on the time adverb *tonight*
4 a habitual action; the meaning here depends on the adverb *always*.

C All the utterances contain, or consist of, verbs in the imperative form, expressing something different each time:

1 an instruction   4 a supplication
2 an invitation   5 a standard response to thanks
3 an order   6 advice.

D All the utterances refer to the future, but the verb forms differ and the shades of meaning differ:

1 a parting greeting, short for *I'll see you* which implies that the parties concerned will meet again soon, in the normal course of events
2 part of a pre-arranged programme (futurity expressed by *due to* and the time)
3 an expectation (near future expressed by *about to*)
4 statement about the future (train departure) based on known facts (a regular timetable)
5 expression of intention (*going to …*)
6 this could be his intention, or merely a neutral statement of what lies ahead of him – the futurity is expressed only by the time phrase *in June* – note the change of meaning if these words are omitted!
7 this is an unalterable fact about the future – often called the **pure** future, expressed by *shall/will*.

E Each utterance contains an element of hypothesis, differing in situation and time reference:

1 a piece of advice; the speaker uses the common device of putting himself/herself in the listener's place
2 … but the listener is still there, therefore the *unreal* element
3 … but you're not!
4 … but he didn't (and so failed his exams)
5 … but no one did.

The verb forms correspond to the subjunctive in many other languages – they *look* like past tense verbs but in meaning are not related to the past. For further treatment of this topic, see section 7 (pp 16–17, 71–2).

F Each utterance expresses a degree of possibility or probability, differing in degree:

1 very improbable
2 possible
3 self-explanatory
4 certain
5 probable.

For a fuller treatment of this topic see section 12 (pp 23–4, 77–9).

3 Tense and time

NB Initial trainees may find this exercise puzzling and will need guidance. See G. Leech and J. Svartvik *A Communicative Grammar of English* (Longman) pp74–5 for a diagrammatic representation of tense/time relationships. This is an initial sensitization exercise; most of the problems raised receive more detailed treatment in subsequent exercises.

A 1 g d e c f a b is the likeliest order The essential clues are in the verb forms, in the time expressions and in the overall context which is gradually built up by associating the utterances with each other and with the speaker.

2 (a)3, (b)7, (c)1, (d)2, (e)5, (f)6, (g)4.

B 1 Present time is usually expressed by present tenses; present tenses may, however, be used in combination with future time expressions, to express future time.

2 This is generally true; the *pastness* is signalled by the form of the verb and the time is specified when necessary, in an adverbial phrase.

3 This certainly is not true, and early attempts to write grammars of English on the lines of Latin grammars resulted in some persistent misunderstandings about how the English verb system works, eg over the existence of a future *tense*, and the meanings accorded to various forms of the past. In fact the *forms* of our verbs have Germanic, rather than Latin, origins.

4 and 5 American linguists assure us that the Hopi Indians lack time concepts, but as few learners of English live in such social and cultural isolation, it is safe to assume that most speakers of other languages perceive time in much the same ways as we do. Difficulties are caused for the foreign learner less because of perceptual problems than because different languages express time concepts in different ways, eg the present perfect in German expresses much of what is expressed in the simple past in English; Chinese has no varying verb forms – time differences are expressed by adverbial particles. Speakers of Arabic, when speaking of the future, usually add the proviso 'God willing', an example of religious belief affecting the way time is perceived and expressed in a language.

6 Occasionally it is the only time marker, but there is almost always

reinforcement in the form of a time adverbial. Thus, speakers of languages with highly inflected verb systems, eg French, Spanish, Russian, often underrate the importance of these adverbial phrases and omit them.

4 Questions

A Questions requiring *yes* or *no* answers: 3, 5, 7, 9, 11
Questions requiring information in the answer: 1, 2, 4, 6, 8, 10, 12

Another possibility would be:
Questions beginning with a question word: 1, 2, 4, 6, 10, 12
Questions formed by subject/verb inversion: 3, 5, 7, 8, 9, 11

B Questions asking for information: 1, 5, 9
Questions expecting a negative reply: 2, 4, 7 (perhaps!), 11
Requests: 3, 8
Questions expecting a positive reply: 6, 7 (perhaps!), 13, 14
Offers: 10, 12

The questions could also be grouped eg into those **with** and those **without** tag questions. Questions can have many functions and it is not enough merely to teach the rules about inversion and the use of *do/does/did*.

C 1 Learner has not absorbed the fact that the main verb reverts to infinitive after *do/does/did*. This may only be apparent in the 3rd person singular of the present simple which differs from the infinitive form through the extra *-s*.
2 Learner has not modified the word order. Difficulty arises over the difference between *aren't I* (a mystery anyway!) and *am I not*.
3 Same problem as in 1 above, except that the verb is now in the simple past.
4 Learner has failed to absorb the rule about question formation with *do/does*. The chances are that his/her mother tongue forms questions by direct inversion of subject and main verb.
5 Overgeneralization. Learner has wrongly applied to an auxiliary verb *can* what he knows about question formation with *do/does*.
6 Learner has chosen the main verb instead of the auxiliary to form the tag question.
7 Learner has not grasped that *shall* in questions is usually only used with the first person singular and plural. The mistake may be one of false analogy; the learner may have heard *Shall I ...?* and generalized from it.
8 Learner has wrongly identified *better* as the auxiliary preceding *go* and has creatively formed his/her own tag question. This error is common among native speaker children.

D 1 The polite greeting (which normally requires an identical reply) has been mistaken for a genuine enquiry about health.
2 This is a common error! The polite enquiry about health (seldom answered honestly by an Englishman!) has been mistaken for a standard greeting requiring an identical reply.

3 The *can* of the question has been understood to refer to **ability**; in fact the question is a request for **assistance**. English speakers sometimes deliberately misunderstand *can* questions in this way!

4 The question has been mistakenly understood as referring to the present moment; the *do* should be received as a signal denoting a question about habit or routine.

5 The questioner wanted reassurance. The impatient reply shows that the speaker has interpreted the question as expressing lack of confidence in his ability to finish the work.

In each case, the **function** of the question has not been understood, though there is obvious familiarity with the **forms**.

E   Context would dictate appropriate intonation which would in turn give the listener the clue as to the function of each question, but these are the most likely choices: 1(e), 2(a), 3(h), 4(b), 5(f), 6(c), 7(d), 8(i), 9(j), 10(g).

The exercise demonstrates the vital role of **intonation** in determining function.

F   1   Maybe because the teacher does too much questioning and does not give his learners sufficient opportunity to initiate communication. Maybe because the forms with *do*, *did*, etc *are* difficult to master.

2   The word *interrogative* describes the grammatical form which is used to ask a *question*. The rules for the formation of interrogatives are fairly easily assimilated and can be committed to memory; learners need to know when and how to ask the **question** appropriate to their communicative needs.

5   Future time

A   1   *I'll help* ... expresses an offer of assistance.
2   *will* (when stressed) expresses irritation at a bad habit.
3   ... *will you* ... expresses a request (familiar or slightly impatient).
4   *Shall I* ... expresses an offer of assistance.
5   This is **pure future**.
6   *Shall we* ... expresses a suggestion.
7   This one is marginal. It may be seen as **pure future** or as expressing inevitability (to be interpreted as a threat or warning).
8   *will* ... expresses the resigned attitude of the speaker to a universally accepted state of affairs.
9   *will* is required after *think* in a request for an opinion about the future.
10   *shall* expresses insistence, the imposing of an obligation.
11   This is **pure future**.

Shall and *will* are comparatively rarely used with **pure future meaning**, which means that it could be very confusing to refer to them as **the future tense**. They are very frequently used to express an *attitude* (willingness, insistence, resignation, etc).

B The examples show how rarely we talk completely dispassionately about the future. The past is the past and can't be changed. When we talk about the future, however, we often express ourselves personally – in this exercise there are examples of expressions of hope, probability, intention and possibility as well as the more neutral future expressed in 1 and 9.

C 1 Not acceptable. *Shall* is seldom used in normal **statements** in spoken English as the short forms *I'll* and *we'll* are preferred. But it is still needed in interrogative forms *Shall I …?* and *Shall we …?*
  2 Not acceptable. *Will* is, in fact, often used with first persons, and *shall* can be used with the second person to express insistence (*You **shall** do it!*).
  3 Acceptable, with the exception of interrogatives, for reasons stated in 1 above.
  4 Grammar books are inevitably behind the times. There are still teachers of English who **insist** on *shall* in all first person statements, but to do this is to ignore trends in the language.
  5 *Shall* should be taught when it is needed, ie to help in the expression of suggestions (*Shall we go for a walk?*) and offers of help (*Shall I open it for you?*), but not merely for the sake of formal completeness when the future is being taught.

  The majority of these statements also apply to *should* and *would,* though it is worth noting that *should* is very commonly used to give advice or impose obligations (eg *You should see a doctor* or *You should work harder*).

D Some teachers would teach *shall/will* first as it is most commonly identified as, and associated with, the future.

  Others would go for the present continuous plus time adverb as this does not entail learning a new structure. *Going to* also has the present continuous form and is useful in expressions of intention and probability. Choice of which to teach first will depend on many factors, eg mother tongue of learners, the type of English they need, etc.

6 Voice

A In shop windows, restaurants, etc in tourist areas. French, German and Spanish all use **active** constructions with impersonal forms. English uses the passive. This is typical of the preference English has for the passive in impersonal expressions.

B 1 Notice (written) in a supermarket. Use of passive shows that it is written, not spoken. Word *customers* comes first to catch the eye.
  2 Car owner contacting police or talking to someone about theft of his/her car. Car dominates his/her thought and is mentioned first. Name of thief not known and not relevant to what the owner wants to express at this stage.
  3 News bulletin or newspaper article. The high number of people is shocking and comes first. The passive helps to emphasize this; at this stage, the name of the person who **reported** this is irrelevant.
  4 Reply to a question like *Where's your car?* Name of person repairing the car is irrelevant here; interest centres on the car.

5 Admonition to make sure the listener knows the consequences of an action. The use of the passive adds formality, weight and distance to the statement.

6 Notice. (eg on building site, private estate). No one is interested in who does the prosecuting – the emphasis is on the fate awaiting trespassers.

7 Newspaper headline. Name of assassin probably not yet known and Hani is the focal point of the article.

C It is written too loosely and informally. The title is *Oxygen* and this should generally be the subject. It could be rewritten as follows:

Oxygen
Oxygen was first prepared by Joseph Priestley in 1774. He prepared it by heating mercuric oxide but nowadays it is produced commercially in large quantities by a process called fractional distillation. It is contained in both air and water and is given off by plants in their respiratory process.

(The use of the passive ensures focus on *Oxygen* as the central theme and cuts down on the number of repetitions of *it*, which makes the original version sound so clumsy.)

D The exercise is futile because (a) there is no communicative point in turning active sentences into the passive and (b) the passive is simply not appropriate to all the examples, especially 1 and 2.

It also encourages production of tautologies such as: 'Our house was broken into *by somebody* last night'. The **agent** is superfluous here as (presumably) animals and birds do not burgle houses!

E 1 The first one implies that boredom drove them home. The second one implies that all work had been completed and there was nothing more in need of attention.

2 The first one implies that Scotland offers little interest to the visitor. The second one implies that the streets are empty of people.

F All these verbs are normally used in the passive rather than the active voice, a fact made clearer in each case by the absence of an **agent**.

G 1 The passive formalizes and depersonalizes the warning.

2 The passive lets the PM off the hook. Politicians often use it to avoid the consequences of being directly quoted – in this example the PM expresses optimism without giving the required undertaking which he might later regret.

3 The passive allows the spokesman to make a non-committal statement, designed to discourage further questioning.

4 The professor's use of the passive focuses attention on the real author and emphasizes the student's mistake to him.

5 Fred is able to take up his questioner's interest in Joe by choosing the passive, which allows Joe to remain the subject of the sentence.

H 1 The use of the passive in newspaper headlines allows emphasis on the **patient** (ie the person or thing affected by an action), which is often at the centre of interest in news stories.

2 In this passage, the focus is on the process of cheese-making. The passive is often used to describe processes, when the focus is on the **product** rather than on the producer.

3 This textbook extract shows a switch from a fairly **personal** style ('...we said ... we use', etc) to a much more impersonal description of the use and composition of transformers. This switch from informal/personal to formal/detached is emphasized by the authors' switch from active to passive voice at the beginning of the second paragraph.

I 1 In the first sentence, he paid someone to do it for him; in the second, he repaired it himself.

2 In the first sentence, the subject wants to pay someone to develop the film for him. The second sentence is a more neutral question and does not necessarily imply an immediate desire for the service.

3 There is a shift of emphasis here, too. The first one implies an arrangement with the dentist; the second is a simple statement of fact.

J The sentences would need to be completed on these lines:

1 ... *do you have it cut?*
2 ... *do you have it done?*
3 ... *do you have it delivered?*
4 ... *do you have them made?*
5 ... *do you have it cleaned?*

As an exercise requiring some initiative, it is acceptable. As a drill, it falls down as the information in the first part is not always adequate to allow correct completion. Despite this, there is enough context for a learner to be able to begin to associate the form (sometimes known as the **causative**) with the meaning.

7 Conditionals and hypothetical meaning

A The verb forms in *italic* all have the appearance of past tenses (with the exception of *would rain* in the first sentence), but do not carry any past meaning. In fact they all express something hypothetical, and are better termed **subjunctive** forms than past tense forms as the use of the word *past* in this connection is confusing. The subjunctive is obvious only in the first person of *to be* (*If I were...*) as in 4.

B 1 (b), 2 (c), 3 (a).

C 1 and 9 – *would* as past form of *will* to maintain sequence of tenses after *think* and *was hoping*.
2, 4, 6, 10 – all have an element of hypothesis.
3 and 8 – *would* makes the requests sound polite.
5 and 7 – *would* expresses habit – it is typical of you to forget your keys, and Queen Victoria very seldom smiled.

Note the different time reference in each case, however: the clues are provided by context. There are other possible groupings, but these suffice to show the wide range of meaning of *would* as an auxiliary.

The terms *conditional tense* and *conditional sentences* are common headings in grammars and course books. But there is no real conditional **tense** in English, only expressions of conditional or hypothetical **meaning**. It is more useful to speak of conditional **sentences,** though textbooks often confusingly refer to a sequence of tenses in sentences such as 4 and 8, insisting that a **conditional tense** must be used in the main clause whereas the verb in the subordinate clause should be in the **past tense**. It is almost certainly easier for foreign learners to become familiar with *would* as a commonly used auxiliary with many different meanings, one of which is to express conditions.

D Sentences 2, 4, 6, 11, 12 (possibly) express developments which are certain to take place if a condition is fulfilled – and there seems a strong likelihood in each instance that the condition **will** be fulfilled.

1, 5, 7, 9, 12 (possibly), 13 express much more unlikely developments as the condition in each case is unlikely to be fulfilled. In sentence 1, the speaker seems unlikely to have more time; in sentence 5, the speaker can never actually change his identity; in sentence 7, the speaker is clearly not terribly optimistic about the chances of his friend giving up smoking, etc.

3, 8, 10 deal with the past. In each case the speaker or writer looks back on a past event and states a condition on which things would have turned out differently. It's too late to alter the course of these past events.

Incidentally, these examples show that *if* sentences are not the only means of expressing conditional meaning.

8 Functions

A 1 To indicate that the action was recent and is of current relevance.
2 (a) Suggestion. (b) Suggestion or instruction.
3 Indicates past action and contributes to the formal, impersonal tenor of the utterance.
4 Seeking confirmation of what is hoped for or expected.
5 Indicates purpose.
6 Polite request.
7 Co-ordination and sequence.
8 Indicates future arrangement.
9 Linking two apparently incompatible sentences.
10 Indicating reference back to a house specified in a previous utterance.
11 Contributing to a reasoned refusal or indicating reluctance.
12 Referring back to a previously mentioned topic.
13 Referring to action at a particular point of time in the past.
14 Indicating reaction to a frequent habit.
15 Co-ordination and addition.
16 Expressing polite or qualified disagreement.

B *Function* = job; role; what the word or phrase does in the utterance.

C 1 *Function* = the purpose of the utterance, ie what the speaker/writer intends to achieve through the utterance (eg invite somebody; indicate disagreement). Examples: 2(a) and (b); 2; 4; 6; 11; 14; 16.

 2 *Function* = the information conveyed through the structure (eg the time reference). Examples: 1; 3; 5; 7; 8; 9; 13; 15.
Function 2 is related to **what** the speaker/hearer says whereas function 1 is related to **why** he/she says it.

 3 *Function* = the grammatical role of the utterance (eg reference back to a previous expression; joining two expressions). Examples: 7; 9; 10; 12; 15.

D The potential information of the structure (ie function 2 in C above).

E It relates to the purposes of utterances (ie function 1).

F 1 *A:* Suggestion 4 *A:* Instruction
   B: Refusal   *B:* Query
 2 *A:* Indicating conviction 5 *A:* Advice
   B: Indicating strong disagreement   *B:* Agreement
 3 *A:* Invitation
   B: Acceptance

9 Teaching functions

A 1 They are all ways of expressing disagreement.

 2
Formal	*Semi-formal*	*Informal*
(d), (e), (j), (l)	(a–c), (e), (g), (i), (j), (l), (n)	(c), (e), (f), (h), (i), (l), (n)

Strong	*Definite*	*Tentative*
(h), (m)	(b), (c), (d), (e), (i–l)	(a), (b), (f), (g), (o)

Factual statements	*Opinions*	*Initiating*	*Responding*
(f), (h), (i), (l)	(a–h), (j–n)	(f), (j)	(a–n)

 5 It is important to differentiate between the different exponents of a function and vital that the learner does not regard them as interchangeable as this could lead to misunderstanding and embarrassment.

B 1 The students are merely repeating exponents that they have been taught. They are making no attempt to select the most appropriate exponents and they are disregarding each others' utterances. They are practising the forms of the exponents but they are certainly not practising their use.

 2 The teacher probably listed the exponents of complaining together and the exponents of apologizing together. He/she then probably concentrated on getting students to produce the correct forms of the exponents through imitation and substitution drills. He/she might have exemplified the exponents in situations but he/she certainly has not succeeded in teaching that the exponents are not interchangeable and that each exponent is subtly different from the

others. He/she has probably also encouraged the students to get as many exponents into their dialogue as possible and has not encouraged them to restrict the exponents they use to those that are appropriate to the situation and to the other participants' utterances. When the students performed their impromptu dialogue they could probably see a list of exponents on the board or on a chart.

3 (a) Restrict the exponents you teach.
  (b) Differentiate between the exponents in your teaching.
  (c) Set up practice situations which encourage learners to select exponents appropriate to the situation and to the utterances of the other participant(s).

C 1 It is not real because it consists of a series of interchanges each consisting of request/refusal and each unconnected with the others. It seems to have been designed to practise or elicit as many exponents of request and refusal as possible and ends up giving the impression that the exponents are interchangeable.

There is no consistency of tenor (eg the requests range from very polite to very rude) and the responses are often totally inappropriate (eg a very polite request eliciting a very rude refusal) and the *tone* is often inappropriate to what is being requested (eg *I'd be so grateful if you could find your way to lending me a pen for a minute*).

2 Request and refusal

3 (a) *Request*

Very Polite	*Polite*	*Impolite*
I'd be so grateful if you could possibly find your way to …	Please could you possibly	How about -ing Give me …

(b) *Refusal*

Reluctant	*Definite*
I wish I could but …	I'm broke
If only I could	No way

Reason given	*No reason given*
I'm broke	No way
… it's in the garage	
If only I could	

5 The important criteria for selection are:
  (a) coverage (ie the ability of an exponent to be used instead of others), eg *Could you please … me …* could cover all the other exponents of polite requests.
  (b) frequency (ie how often an exponent is used in everyday situations)
  (c) context frequency (ie how often an exponent is used in particular situations)
  (d) learnability (ie how easy the exponent is to learn), eg *Could you please … me …* is easier to learn than *I'd be so grateful if you could possibly find your way to …*

NB The more exponents that are taught at once, the greater is the danger of confusion. Some exponents should be selected for students to learn to understand and to use; others should be selected only for them to learn to respond to when they are exposed to them.

10 Reporting speech

A 1 Much depends on the intonation and even on the mother's facial expression and body language, but all of these appear possible:

ordering, warning, requesting, persuading, begging, advising, recommending, reminding, insisting, suggesting … and maybe some of the others, too.

2 By listening to the *tone* of her voice, looking at her face, or just by diving in and waiting for her reaction!

3 She ordered him to take his watch off before diving in.

or warned   tried to persuade   advised   requested   begged   reminded

She suggested that he should take his watch off before diving in.

or insisted   recommended

Note that the function is clearer in indirect (or reported) speech, a feature mainly of written English, which is denied the extra dimensions of gesture, facial expression, stress and intonation, all of which help to signal the meaning of a spoken utterance.

B Following on from the conclusions in the previous exercise, it is clearly difficult to decide on the **functions** of many of the twelve utterances, and therefore to choose an appropriate expression in indirect speech. In any case, there is no communicative point to the exercise as it stands. It simply requires learners to apply certain formal rules (eg backshift of tenses and time expressions) without reference to meaning, context or appropriacy. When indirect speech is used in written English, it is most often in connected prose and the exercise consists of twelve unrelated examples giving no practice in connected writing.

C 1 There are examples of both direct and indirect speech in the article. Some possible reasons for the writer's choices are:
- stylistic variation;
- choice of direct speech to avoid any risk of *interpretation* or *distortion* of the speaker's actual words;
- choice of indirect speech to generalize or summarize a viewpoint;
- choice of part direct and part indirect speech to combine the previous two criteria;
- choice of indirect 'speech', more usual after verbs such as 'think' and 'believe'.

Other reasons may be identified.

2 The first paragraph seems to be a mixture of reported and direct speech. The absence of inverted commas suggests reported speech, but the medial position of the reporting verb 'insisted' and the choice of 'will' rather than 'would' suggests direct speech. Journalistic licence?

Commentary

D   These conclusions may be mentioned:

- Work on transformations at single sentence level is not enough.
- Rules about form are flexible in real speech and writing.
- Learners need some variation in their range of indirect speech constructions
- Learners need to develop criteria for choosing between direct and indirect speech when writing.

11 Notions

A   1 They all communicate aspects of the notion of duration of time (ie they refer to periods of time).

2 (a) To refer to a complete period of time with either past, present or future time reference. Always followed by an expression referring to a period of time.
   (b) See example.
   (c) To refer to a period of time from a point previously mentioned (or indicated in the situation) to the point of time mentioned immediately after *till*. Can be used with past, present or future time reference and always followed by an expression referring to a point of time.
   (d) As for (c).
   (e) To refer to a lengthy and uninterrupted period of time. Can have past, present or future time reference.
   (f) To refer to what happened continuously during a period of time in the past.
   (g) To refer to what happened continuously during a period of time in the past between two indicated points of time.
   (h) To indicate that a question is being asked about the length of an indicated period of time in the past or future.
   (i) To refer to all of a previously indicated period of time in the past, present or future.
   (j) To indicate the length of a period of time in the past or future.
   (k) To indicate that the opinion is constant.

B   1 They all communicate aspects of the notion of movement.

2 (a) *moved* – indicates movement; *slowly* – indicates speed of movement; *forward* – indicates direction of movement from the starting-point.
   (b) Indicates intended *terminus* of movement.
   (c) Indicates movement from outside to inside.
   (d) *walking* – indicates means of movement; *towards* – indicates direction of movement by reference to a potential *terminus*.
   (e) Indicates movement from inside to outside.
   (f) *ran* – indicates means of movement; *away* – indicates movements which achieve distance; *from* – indicates direction of movement by reference to the starting-point.
   (g) *go* refers to movement from *here*; *fetch* refers to movement from *here* to *there* and then back to *here* again.

4 One possible answer would be:
   (a) means of movement: to walk; to run; to swim; to drive; to travel.

    (b) Speed of movement: slowly; quickly.
    (c) Direction of movement: to, forward(s), backward(s), sideward(s); towards, away, from; into, out of, out.

C 1 eg *The mouse was* inside *this cupboard*; this *is where we will meet on Friday*; it's on *that table.*
    2 Relative position.
    3 Sequence.

D 1 (a) Manner
    (b) Result
    (c) Comparison
    (d) Instrument
    (e) Time

    2 eg *Time*
    (a) *then* = immediately after the previous occurrence mentioned, eg *I put the money in the safe. Then I rang the manager.*
    (b) *meanwhile* = at approximately the same time as the previous occurrence mentioned.
    eg *Mr Carter was operated on at 2 pm. Meanwhile his brother was standing by to give blood if it was required.*
    (c) *While* or *whilst* = at the same time as the previous occurrence mentioned was taking place.
    eg *I papered the living room while my wife painted the kitchen.*
NB *While* relates two continuous actions together in time and usually in place. It joins two clauses (or a clause and a phrase within one sentence).
Meanwhile relates two events together in time and type. It links two sentences together.
eg *I listened to the radio while peeling the potatoes.*
    ✗ *I listened to the radio. Meanwhile I peeled the potatoes.*
So England were convincing winners of the European Championship. Meanwhile in Lima last night Brazil beat Peru to win the South American Championship.
    ✗ *So England were convincing winners of the European Championship while in Lima last night Brazil beat Peru to win the South American Championship.*

12 Modal meaning

A 1(a), 2(a), 3(b), 4(a), 5(b), 6(b), 7(a), 8(b), 9(a), 10(b), 11(b), 12(b), 13(b), 14(b), 15(b).

Of the sentences in which the meaning of the verb is modified, sentence 3 indicates deduction (logical necessity). In 5 *ought to* indicates advice or obligation. In 6 *can't* indicates inability. In 8 *couldn't have* indicates deduction (logical necessity). 10 future meaning. In 11 *will* indicates willingness. In 12 *will have to* indicates future necessity (or obligation). In 13 *is likely to* indicates probability. In 14 *might* indicates possibility. In 15 *it's essential that* indicates an imperative, or strong obligation.

B 1 There are no **right** answers here, and there is certain to be disagreement about which point on the line some of the sentences should be allocated to. This is, in itself, a warning **against** attempts to pin down differences between fine shades of meaning.

   2 There are many views about which sentence types to teach first, but one approach would be to choose three or four points on the scale between *out of the question* and *absolute certainty* and to select the commonest ways of expressing these degrees of meaning. It is worth noting that modal meaning is expressed in many different ways, not just by the use of modal auxiliaries. The simplest way, structurally, is by the addition of a single adverb such as *perhaps, maybe* or *definitely*.

C 1 They are distinguished by their relative formality or informality.

   2 The question of which to teach first ought to be decided by the learners' priorities and the circumstances in which they are most likely to be using English. The most neutral choice is probably *Can I go home now?* though *Could I ...* adds a touch of extra politeness (often an asset for non-native speakers in an English-speaking environment!).

D 1 Expresses likelihood.
   2 Expresses discontinued ability.
   3 Asks permission.
   4 Expresses absence of obligation.
   5 Expresses disapproval or disappointment at failure to do something.
   6 Expresses logical impossibility.
   7 Expresses logical certainty.
   8 Gives permission.
   9 Expresses possibility.
  10 Expresses obligation.

E There are many different ways of expressing each of these. Two or three are given here in each case to ensure that the basic concept is clear:

   1 He *may possibly* come.
      Perhaps he'll come.
      There's *a chance that* he'll come.
   2 She's *capable* of defending herself.
      She *can* defend herself.
      She *has the ability* to defend herself.
   3 You *must* help your father.
      You're *obliged to* help your father.
      It's *your responsibility* to help your father.
   4 You *have to* have a cholera injection if you travel to the Middle East.
      A cholera injection *is required* for travel to the Middle East.
      You *need* a cholera injection if you travel to the Middle East.
   5 He *will* keep grinding his teeth.
      He's *always* grinding his teeth.

In all the examples, note once again how many ways there are of expressing modal meaning other than by auxiliaries.

F 1 *could* is reserved for general ability in the past; *was able* is used with the meaning of *managed to* (usually on a single occasion) but also to express general ability.

2 The first utterance prohibits; the second one removes obligation.

3 We use *should* and *ought to* to impose moral obligations and they are practically interchangeable, though *ought to* is arguably more forceful.

4 There is no significant difference.

5 *I may come* is more likely than *I might come*.

6 *Shall* is used mainly in first person forms, to offer assistance: *Shall I do that for you?*, to make a suggestion: *Shall we go now?*, or in *pure* future statements, interchangeable with *will*: *I shall be 64 next birthday*.
Will is used with all other persons in *pure* future expressions, but also to express willingness: *Will you help me?*; promises: *I will* (in marriage ceremony); offers of help: *I'll do it for you*; and bad habits: *Joe* will *talk with his mouth full*. Learners often make too much of the difference between *shall* and *will* in future statements. In fact, the elided forms, *I'll, we'll, you'll,* etc often make the difference irrelevant. (See also Unit 2, section 5.)

7 (a), in which only *used to* is feasible, expresses a single discontinued habit. (b), in which either *used to* or *would* is possible, expresses one of a number of events or experiences bracketed by a time reference (in this case *When I was a boy*).

13 Auxiliary verbs

A Those underlined twice are main verbs; they contribute meaning to their utterances. Those underlined once are not the main verbs in their clauses; their function is to *help* the main verbs to contribute meaning or to add to the meaning of the main verbs.

B The verbs in the first utterance in each pair are main verbs whereas those in the second utterance in each case are verbs helping main verbs.

C 1 Those underlined twice are verbs which add to the meaning of the main verb. They usually indicate something about the attitude or opinion of the speaker and are called **modal verbs**. Those underlined once help the main verbs and are called **auxiliary verbs**. Both types of verbs can be used to:

(a) form the interrogative.
(b) form the negative
(c) stand for the main verb in short form responses (eg (e) and (j))
(d) stand for the main verb in question tags.

In addition those underlined once (ie auxiliary verbs) are used to help form tenses and to help indicate number and person (eg *I have been/He has been; he is playing/they are playing*).

2 Other modal verbs are: should; has to; will; might; would; dare.

D *has* – helping to form the present perfect tense of the modal auxiliary verb (… an auxiliary)
had to – adding to the meaning of the main verb (… a modal)
have – main verb.

E (a) Helping to form the tense of the main verb. (nos. 1, 2, 3, 4, 5, 6, 7, 8, 9, 10)

(b) Forming the negative of the main verb (2, 3, 4, 7, 10)

(c) Forming the interrogative of the main verb (1, 6, 8, 10)

(d) Standing for the main verb in:

short form answers (1, 8)

short form responses (2, 10)

question tags (4, 7, 9)

(e) Helping to indicate the person of the subject (ie first, second or third) (2, 3, 4, 5, 7, 8, 9, 10)

(f) Helping to indicate the number of the subject (ie singular or plural) (5, 8, 9).

F 1 (a) Was (d) was (g) did (j) was

(b) wasn't (e) did (h) were (k) did

(c) had (f) did (i) had (l) had

2 (a) Yes. To help form the past continuous tense and to help form the interrogative.

(b) Yes. To form the negative and to stand for the main verb.

(c) Yes. To help form the past perfect tense.

(d) No.

(e) Yes. To help form the interrogative and the past simple tense.

(f) Yes. To stand for the main verb and to indicate the past simple tense.

(g) Yes. As for (f).

(h) No.

(i) No.

(j) Yes. To help form the past continuous tense.

(k) Yes. To stand for the main verb (*take*) and to indicate the past simple tense.

(l) Yes. To help form the past perfect tense.

14 *Have* and *be*

A 1 These answers are suggestions only – many alternatives are possible – but note the verb forms.

(a) When did the phone ring?

(b) What were you doing when the phone rang?

(c) Have you got the time?/ Have you finished yet?

(d) Did you have a good time at the circus?

(e) Has he got two brothers?/ He's got two brothers, hasn't he?

(f) What did you have for breakfast this morning?

(g) What sort of car have you got?

(h) What are you doing?

(i) Have you ever been to Japan?

(j) You're having a check-up soon, aren't you?

(k) What have they had, a boy or a girl?

(l) Have you got a light, please?

2 In some cases, *have* functions as a main verb, and in others as an auxiliary.

B   1 *have* here has causative force. Someone is taking his tonsils out *for* him, possibly at his request . (See also Unit 2, section 6, I and J).

2 The assumption is that the person addressed is not always cruel and is capable of changing his/her behaviour.

3 *has* here is a substitute for the (slightly) tautologous *eat*. The verb has positive, dynamic force.

4 … but in a while she'll come to her senses, change her behaviour and be sensible again.

5 *have* here means *accept*.

6 Again, there is causative force here. She has instructed someone to perm her hair for her.

7 Present continuous passive (*is being repainted*) stresses the fact that the process is under way at the time of speaking. *Be* as a passive auxiliary has a dynamic force.

C   1 (b) is unacceptable as *handsome* is a **stative** adjective (it describes a permanent state, in contrast to *careful*, which describes a temporary state).

2 (b) is unacceptable. (a) is an admonition which applies to a single instance and is in the imperative. There is no obvious **behaviour** which is identifiable as *being late* and so this is not acceptable here.

3 (b) is unacceptable for similar reasons to those stated in 1 and 2. Stubbornness may be a permanent trait of character but the statement *She's being stubborn* clearly describes her behaviour in a particular instance. The adjective *beautiful* describes permanent appearance rather than passing behaviour, which makes the continuous form inappropriate.

4 (a) is unacceptable. *Have* with the meaning of *possess* cannot be used in the continuous form. In 4(b) *having* expresses an activity; it could (unlike 4(a)) answer the question *What are you doing?*

5 (b) is unacceptable. You can't *offer* someone a headache!

6 (b) is unacceptable in most contexts. The use of *just* plus present perfect usually indicates a recently completed *action*, as in 6(a), where *had* = *consumed*.

7 (b) is unacceptable in most contexts. *Being British* is not (unless in a mime or charade!) a temporary state of affairs. The use of the present participle in 7(a) is a normal way of introducing a cause/effect relationship in an utterance.

8 (b) would normally not be acceptable. *Has got* is usually used to express possession as in 8(a) though it could also be used in utterances like *She's got an appointment*, though this would normally refer only to a single instance; the addition of *every evening* in 8(b) adds an extra dimension.

9 (b) is clearly unacceptable. Whilst *have*, in its dynamic sense, forms questions and negatives with the auxiliary *do*, *be* does not. The correct version of 9(b) would be simply *I'm not always stupid.*

D Category one (dynamic uses): 1, 3, 8, 9, 10, 11, 12.
Category two (stative uses): 2, 4, 5, 6, 7, 13, 14, 15.

NB In 4 and 6 the stupidity is seen as a permanent characteristic; in 8 it is seen as a temporary state.

E *Be* is used as an auxiliary in 1 and 5 (twice).
Have is used as an auxiliary in 2, 3^1, 7^1 and 9.

F 1 This is a common misconception. *Have got* is absolutely standard in spoken English, and should be taught; however, it is usually avoided in formal written English.

2 The foreign learner has clearly picked up the auxiliary from the command in his short response. He may have been trained to listen for the auxiliary in **questions** to enable him to make the correct short response, but is not yet aware that this does not apply to imperatives. (The fact that the example contains *be* is a distractor here – it could equally well have been *Don't go* or *Don't speak*.)

3 The foreign learner has either been told to avoid *got* or has wrongly used the negative form appropriate to the auxiliary *have*, when this *have* expresses possession.

4 Perhaps the main conclusion is that *be* and *have* have to be *recycled* at intervals. Attention then has to be drawn to the distinct meanings and their grammatical consequences. It is significant that there is *no dynamic use* of *be* and *have* in most other languages. Compare
He's having breakfast with
Er frühstückt gerade (German) or
Il prend son petit déjeuner (French);
and
She's being silly with
Sie spinnt (German) or
Elle fait des bêtises (French).

15 Comparisons

A All of them contain implicit or explicit comparisons or contrasts usually between two ideas or objects.

1 Expresses a straightforward comparison (of length) between two rivers.

2 Expresses a contrast between two newspapers; an explanation of one aspect in which they differ.

3 Expresses a contrast between two types of coal.

4 A direct comparison of intelligence between Willy and his brother, this time expressed negatively.

5 There is an implicit contrast and comparison between the two flats.

6 A comparison of hair colour, revealing *sameness* rather than *difference*.

7 … that is, more clearly than you are doing! A comparison between the present way of speaking and the wished-for way.

8 A comparison of character between two brothers, using a noun *extrovert* rather than a descriptive adjective.

9 A comparison of membership numbers between the AA and other motoring organizations.

10 Comparison between an actual and an ideal state of affairs.

11 A comparison between degrees of happiness as a way of setting an ideal to aim at.

12 This is almost a platitude which equates an increase in enjoyment. The comparison is proportionate.

13 A comparison for effect, between existing weather conditions and *ice*, representing the ultimate in cold.

14 Another platitude, comparing an achievement with an optimum standard.

There are, as these examples show, many ways of expressing comparison and contrast, and it is not sufficient to deal with the topic under the restricted structural heading (common in textbooks) *Comparative and superlative of adjectives and adverbs.*

B 1 This exercise provides practice in the comparative and superlative **forms** of adjectives without giving any consideration to the **function** of comparing or to different ways of comparing.
  (a) heavy – heavier (two syllables, ending in -y, compare *easy, happy*)
  (b) difficult – more difficult (more than two syllables, cf *intelligent, important*)
  (c) old – older (monosyllabic adjective, cf *young, long, short*)
  (d) careful – more careful (two or more syllables, compound adjective, cf *beautiful, helpful, thoughtless*)
  (e) fast – faster (monosyllabic adverb, cf *hard*)
  (f) obedient – more obedient (cf (b) above)
  (g) high – highest (superlative of monosyllabic adjective, cf *short, long, wide*)
  (h) beautiful – most beautiful (superlative of compound adjective, two or more syllables, cf *thoughtful, plentiful*)
  (i) far – farther/further (irregular comparative form)
  (j) bad – worse (irregular comparative form)

  2 The rules which can be deduced concern the different ways of **forming** the comparative of adjectives.

16 Tense and function 1

A 1 *got* = past simple = indicating action at a specific time and place in the past.
  had gone = past perfect = indicating action which occurred before the other action referred to.
  2 *was walking* = past continuous = indicating continuous action in the past.
  saw = simple past = indicating event at a specific time and place in the past.
  3 *will have finished* = future perfect = indicating future event which will have finished before another event (mentioned in the utterance or indicated in the situation) takes place.
  have finished = present perfect = indicating action which will occur after another action in the future.
  4 *you're* = simple present = indicating present state.
  's gone home = present perfect = indicating action in recent past with present relevance.
  5 *see* = indicating present state.
  got arrested = simple past = indicating action at specific time in the past.
  6 *walked* = simple past = indicating action at specific time in the past.
  worked = simple past = indicating period of time in the past.
  7 *comes* = simple present = indicating future action.
  will let ... know = future simple (or modal + main verb) = indicating present decision about a future action.
  8 *does leave* = simple present = indicating usual routine.
  's gone = present perfect = indicating an event in the recent past with present relevance.

9 *'ve been waiting* = present perfect continuous – indicating an event with continuation from a point in the past to the present.

10 *meet* = simple present = indicating past formal arrangement about the future.

11 *has come* = present perfect – indicating an action in the recent past with current relevance.

B 1 From the choice of the past perfect and from *already*.

2 It would indicate that the walking only started after Mary had been seen.

3 (a) Because of the convention of *will* not being used in time clauses unless it is used to indicate willingness.

(b) No.

(c) Yes. It would indicate that a regular state of affairs is being referred to.

4 No. The *just* and the *too late* indicate recent past and suggest present relevance.

5 *See* could be put into the simple past without seriously interfering with the message; *has got arrested* would be grammatically wrong but reference to a specific past action would still be indicated by *yesterday*.

6 The *every day* and the *when* are strong enough to indicate past habit even if an inappropriate tense was used.

eg ✗ *He has walked to work every day when he worked at the station in 1968.*

7 No. The use of the simple present in time clauses with future relevance is a convention. The future reference would still be communicated by the *will let* even if other tenses were used.

eg ✗ *When he will come I will let you know.*

✗ *When he came I will let you know.*

8 No. Pointing to the departing train is sufficient to indicate recent past and present relevance regardless of the tense used.

eg ✗ *It just went.*

✗ *It had just gone.*

9 Yes. The present perfect (ie *I've waited here for thirty minutes*).

10 (a) That a formal arrangement has already been made.

(b) That the arrangement is for a specific time in the future.

11 Not very important. The *yet* is strong enough to indicate recent past and present relevance.

C 1 change the meaning

2 function … another expression … something in the situation.

3 … meaning of the utterance … utterance … situation … meaning … clear … appropriacy … function … cause the utterance to be misunderstood.

D

1	2	3
was walking (2)	got (1)	have finished (3)
're late (4)	had gone (1)	's gone home (4)
will let you know (7)	saw (2)	got arrested (5)
does leave (8)	will have finished (3)	worked (6)
meet (10)	see (5)	comes (7)
	walked (6)	's gone (8)
	've been waiting (9)	has come (11)

H 2 *had slept* – the selection of the past perfect is crucial as it is the only indicator that the child no longer slept there.

3 *had been shifted* – the selection of the past perfect is crucial as it is the only indicator that the shifting took place before the arrival of the writer.

4 *called* – the choice of the past simple is important as it helps to indicate that the room had not been called that before. However, the crucial word is *now* and its force could survive an erroneous choice of tense.

5 *lay* – the tense contrasts with the past perfect of the previous sentence and indicates that this was true at that particular time in the past that the writer is describing. However, the past continuous, the present simple or the present continuous could have been used without changing the meaning of the utterance.

6 *had ... succeeded* – the choice of the past perfect again indicates that this happened before the time that is being described.

7 *was lying* – the choice of the past continuous indicates that this was true at the time the writer is describing. However, the simple past could have been used without interfering with the grammar or the meaning of the utterance. The simple present and present continuous would have been ungrammatical in contrast with the past perfect but would nevertheless have communicated the same meaning.

I 1 *it is* – the simple present indicates it is true now. No other tense could have been used.

2 *'s been* – the present perfect indicates that this has been true from a point in the past until now. The simple past could also have been used.

3 *'ve been looking* – the present perfect continuous indicates a continuous action from a point of time in the past until now. The past continuous could have been used with the same function and the simple past and the present perfect, although not grammatically appropriate in this utterance, could have been used without interfering with the message being communicated.

4 *'ll take* – this indicates that a decision is being made now about the future. No other tense would be grammatically acceptable but the situation would probably make this clear if any other tense with potential future reference was used.

5 *'m meeting* – the present continuous indicates that an arrangement has been made in the past for the future. The situation and the *at nine* make the future reference clear but the tense is crucial as an indication of previous arrangement.

6 *'ll give* – as for 4.

7 *was going* – the past continuous indicates a past intention for the future which no longer applies. No other tense could have been used without interfering with the meaning of the utterance.

8 *'s ringing* – the present continuous is used to indicate present duration. No other tense would be grammatically acceptable but the situational signal (ie the actual ringing) is so strong that the meaning of the utterance would still be clear if other tenses were used by mistake.

9 *'ll get* – this indicates a present decision about the immediate future. Again the situational signals are so strong that effective communication would probably take place whatever tense was used.

10 *rings* – the simple present is used to indicate that this is a habit. However *usually* and *about this time* are such strong signals of habit that the choice of an inappropriate tense would probably not interfere with communication.

11 *'s stopped* – the present perfect indicates the recent past. However, the situation would probably make the meaning clear regardless of what tense was used.

12 *didn't answer* – the simple past refers to a point of time in the past. The situation would allow the inappropriate present perfect and even the incorrect past perfect to be used without serious danger of misapprehension.

J The following points could be made:

1 The learners do not have to be able to use all the tenses to communicate all their functions as often more than one tense can be used to communicate the same function in the same situation.

2 It is important when teaching the function of a tense to exemplify the use of that tense in utterances which would not permit other tenses to be used and still communicate the same meaning (eg the past perfect should be exemplified in utterances in which it is not interchangeable with the simple past).

3 Often the learner can get away with using the wrong tense if his intended function is communicated by other features of the utterance (eg *just, usually, often, tomorrow, for, yet, already, every day*). Considerable teaching time should be devoted to those items (mainly adverbials) which can reinforce and sometimes even replace the functional signals of tense.

4 The teacher should be selective in his correction of tense error. Those errors which frustrate communication (eg *I had given it to him when you told me to* instead of, *I gave it to him when you told me to*) are more serious than those which do not (eg ✗ *I'll tell you before the lesson* will *finish*).

17 Tense and aspect

A Category one (single events or repeated actions): 1, 4, 5, 7.
Category two (actions spanning a named or implied point in time): 2, 3, 6, 8.

B 1 The question aims to elicit the learner's reaction to the telephone ringing. He misunderstands it as an enquiry about what he *was doing* when it rang. He is not sensitive to the clearly stated *simple* aspect of the question *What did you do…?* This is a very common error. (An obvious answer would be *I answered it.*)

2 The learner wrongly selects a continuous form to express a habit. (Better: *I don't smoke.*)

3 The learner is not aware that stative verbs, and particularly verbs expressing feelings or emotions, are not usually used in the continuous form unless a change of meaning is involved.
Compare:
What do *you* think *of the government?* (enquiry about general attitude) – *I think it's awful.*
with:
What are *you* thinking *about?* (emphasis on process *at the moment*) – I'm thinking *about my girlfriend.*
Most grammars have lists of verbs of this type with notes on uses and restrictions.

4 The question *Will you go to the post office?* would be interpreted as a definite request, and sounds rather blunt and inappropriate here. The learner almost certainly intends to make a more neutral enquiry: *Will you be going to the post office?* (in the course of your visit to town); the future continuous in this type of context is seldom mastered even by the most advanced foreign learners as it is difficult to account for in structural terms.

5 The learner misunderstands the question as an enquiry about his reaction to the doorbell ringing. Again, a frequent mistake. (Better: *I was having dinner.*)

6 The learner has simply not internalized the fact that we use the simple past tense when talking about finished time; many other languages use the present perfect in such cases, making it doubly confusing. (Better: *Where were you last night?*)

7 A common misconception about the past perfect (here: *had built*) is that it is used to refer to the *very* distant past. In fact it is used to provide an extra dimension in the past (however recent or distant) when there is already one point of reference expressed by the simple past.
eg *I had been asleep for quite a while when you* came *in.*
In the example given, the learner could have answered in the simple past.

C Many of these examples illustrate the confusion between tense and aspect which underlie the thinking of many learners – the present *continuous* (or progressive), for example is best thought of as an aspect of the present tense, not as a separate tense, especially since few other languages have corresponding verb forms and use adverbs or other means to express continuous aspect. It helps learners if the teacher stresses the conceptual links between continuous aspects of different tenses, eg
I'm working in London now,
This time five years ago *I was working* in Paris,
This time next year *I'll be working* in Rome,
rather than dealing with each tense and aspect in isolation.
It is essential for teachers to familiarize themselves with the complexities of tense and aspect in a good grammar if they are not to confuse their learners.

18 Tense and function 2

A 1 This is not true. Examples of the most obvious exceptions are: *I've just repaired the car* (the action is complete) and *I had only just repaired the car when it broke down again* (past perfect used to express the time relationship between the repairing and the second breakdown).
In fact, the simple past tense is used when the time of an action is specified or clearly known.

2 This is a half truth. It is certainly true to say that the present continuous form often occurs in statements about the future, but it does not itself express the future. Compare *I'm watching TV* with *I'm watching TV later this evening.* These continuous forms are identical; without a future time expression, the first example must be taken as referring to the present moment. In fact, the continuous form is almost certainly used more often in association with future meaning than as a description of an action in progress at the time of speaking.

However, it is the time expression, not the verb form, which gives the second utterance its future meaning.

3 This is an oversimplification based on attempts to establish *shall/will* and infinitive as direct equivalents of future tenses in more highly inflected Latin-based languages such as French and Spanish. Most people now seem to agree that there is no single future *tense* in English, just a number of ways of referring to future *time*. (See section 5 above for a fuller treatment of this topic.)

4 This is a very common misconception among learners of English. The past perfect may be used, if appropriate, about the very recent past as readily as about the distant past, eg *She had already finished her supper when her parents came in* (could refer to almost any time).

5 Many languages operate a much stricter sequence of tenses, particularly in writing, than English does. In informal use, a mixing of present and past in the same sentence is perfectly possible, and it may enable the speaker to say what she/he means, eg
I think he played yesterday (acceptable in any case).
He said he plays every week (stresses the regularity; the activity is presumably *still* repeated every week).

B 1 The present continuous tense is not normally used to express habits, but association with an adverb such as *always* or *continually* lends it this meaning, usually expressing a *persistent* habit.

2 The present simple seems out of place with the past adverb *yesterday* – this must be a caption under a newspaper photograph where such an apparently paradoxical association is possible.

3 The present simple expresses the immediacy of an action in a direct commentary on a sports event.

4 The present simple refers to the (future) departure time of a train or bus, possibly though not necessarily following a regular timetable.

5 Both tenses refer to the future, though the second verb is in the present simple because it follows the time conjunction *until*.

6 The present simple expresses a timeless scientific truth.

7 Past simple because the speaker knows Caruso to be dead.

8 Present perfect because the speaker knows Dylan to be alive and so may still go to one of his concerts.

9 Past simple because (a) Hemingway is dead, and (b) the writing of *The Old Man and the Sea* is clearly complete.

10 Dickens is dead, hence the past simple.

11 The directing of *Paris Texas* is complete, hence the past simple. The fact that Wenders is still alive is irrelevant.

12 Present perfect because Drabble is still alive and may write more novels.

13 This was a habit of Gladstone's during the known period of his lifetime (he is now dead) – this accounts for the use of *would*. *Used to* would also be possible here.

14 This, too, is a past habit. Compare *I smoke* (present habit) and *I used to smoke* (discontinued habit). *Used to* in this case supplies the true past of the present simple expressing habit. *Would* would not be possible here.

C 1 The learner has mistakenly assumed that the defective verb *used to*, with its clear past form, has a regular present form.

2 Mistaken use of the simple present with the time expression *for six years*. In many languages (eg French and German), the present simple *is* used where we use the present perfect. The coverage of the concepts expressed by these verb forms varies from one language to another. The confusion may be understood if the present simple and present perfect are each seen as *aspects* of the present tense.

3 Wrong use of simple past to express a (possibly) uncompleted action. (This usage is however common in American English.)

4 Wrong use of present perfect with time adverb *yesterday* which clearly specifies the time of an action in the past, requiring the simple past.

5 Wrong use of past perfect based on the false assumption that this form expresses events in the distant past.

D There are enough clues to make each choice clear and unambiguous, but the six sentences are unconnected. There is no practice in context. The learner knows immediately what is required of him and will probably have little difficulty, on the evidence supplied, in getting these examples right, but will the learner be able to produce the appropriate verb forms in spontaneous speech when they are required? Textbooks abound with this type of gap-fill exercise and yet mistakes are still made. Perhaps there is *overconcentration* on verb forms, resulting in a kind of verb neurosis in many learners.

E Suggested matching (other interpretations may be possible, depending on context). 1(d), 2(g), 3(b), 4(c), 5(a), 6(f), 7(e), 8(h). A possible order of priority for teaching on a 'General English' course would be: 5, 1, 7, 8, 4, 3, 6, 2; 5 and 1 are conceptionally easy, most likely to correspond to usage in the learner's mother tongue, and are fairly frequently needed in *social* English.

19 Non-finite verb forms

A 1 noun, noun
2 verb
3 verb, adjective
4 noun (in fact *going to the dentist's* is a noun phrase, and is the direct object here)
5 noun
6 verb
7 adjective
8 verb
9 verb
10 verb, verb

The verbs and adjectives are all participles. The nouns are gerunds.

B 1 (Several alternatives are suggested in each case; there are many more, of course.)
(a) *silver/broken/new* (all adjectives)
(b) *dull/acclaimed/good* (all adjectives)
(c) my *dinner/ the weekend/ a quiet evening* (all nouns)
(d) *fresh/frozen/delicious* (all adjectives)
(e) *small meals/the dark/so much noise* (all nouns)
(f) *that noise/the fight/work* (all nouns)
2 The *-ing* forms in 1, 2 and 4 are participles and in 3, 5 and 6 gerunds.

C 1 The first example explains why he stopped whatever he was doing. The second one states what he stopped doing.

2 The first example is a reminder. The second asks whether the act can be recalled.

3 Both have the same meaning. The second example is more usual in American English.

4 The first example is a general enquiry. The second is an invitation.

5 The first example expresses the fact that she saw the whole action; the second states that she saw the burglar while he was climbing through the window though she did not necessarily see the action from beginning to end.

6 The first example expresses the speaker's regret (retrospectively) at having told him. The second expresses regret felt at the time of speaking at having to break the bad news.

D All of the errors have to do with inappropriate use of gerund (for infinitive) or infinitive (for gerund).

1 He has great difficulty in speaking English *or* He finds it very difficult to speak English (error probably rooted in mother tongue).

2 I enjoyed visiting Cambridge yesterday (error probably results from false analogy or mother tongue interference).

3 He's going to bed late *or* He used to go to bed late. (These two distinct forms are commonly confused, often as a result of contrastive teaching.)

4 I'm looking forward to hearing from you. (The *to*, in fact a preposition here, has the unfortunate effect of attracting an incorrect infinitive.)

5 He tried *to start* his car … (The change of meaning which results from the use of a gerund instead of an infinitive after *try* is not familiar to the speaker. *My watch has stopped. Try shaking it* – the act is not physically difficult; this is a suggestion; and *Try to concentrate* – make an effort.)

6 I've always been interested in taking … (This indicates a general interest, such as a hobby; if I was interested *to read* the review of a new book, this indicates a single occasion or focus of interest.)

7 I don't feel like going … (false analogy or mother tongue interference).

8 I'm very pleased to see you (probably a straight confusion).

NB Foreign learners find the **gerund** v **infinitive** problem extremely difficult. One reason is because textbooks often deal with it in a single chapter or unit and then regard it as *taught*. In fact, it is best dealt with as it arises, in context, and learners should be encouraged to note down whole constructions, including gerund or infinitive, and not just single words.

20 Adverbs and adjectives

A (Many variations possible.)

1 What colour is your pullover?

2 What colour pullover do you want? Is that a blue pullover or a green one?

3 Which pullover do you want?

4 How does he drive?

5 How often do you go dancing?

6 Does he dance well or badly?

7 What sort of a dancer is he?

8 Where does he live?

B 1 Two possible explanations. The utterance could read either *Sally works hard* or *Sally hardly works*. If the former is intended, the speaker has wrongly assumed that *hardly* is the regular adverb form of *hard*. If the second is intended, the mistake is one of word order.

2 Again two possible explanations. Either the mistake is one of word order (corrected, this would become *My friend speaks English very well*) or it is an adjective/adverb confusion (the correct version would be *My friend speaks very good English*).

3 Probably false analogy with *How are you? I'm fine.* Corrected version: *What's the weather like?* (This could also be an error caused by interference from the mother tongue.)

4 May not be immediately perceived as an error. Learner has not grasped that *far*, while frequent in questions and negatives, is not usually used in straightforward statements of this sort. Corrected version: *Aberdeen is a very long way from London.*

5 Learner has not realized that *ill* cannot normally be used attributively (ie before the noun) with this meaning (ie sick). Corrected version: *I've just been to visit my sick friend.*

6 Incorrect use of adverb in a position normally occupied by an adjective. Corrected version: *That's not a very usual colour for a car.*

7 *Elder* used predicatively (ie after the verb to describe the subject); usually used only attributively. Corrected version: *My sister is older than I am.*

8 Incorrect adverbial formation. Adjectives already ending in *-ly* usually have a compound adverbial form, eg *in a friendly way*.

C 1 *Poorly* (an adjective meaning *unwell*) has the form (ending in *-ly*) which would normally identify it as an adverb. It also has an unexpected meaning.

2 Here, too, the form is apparently that of an adverb.

3, 4 *Hard* and *tight* here are adverbs with a form indistinguishable from that of adjectives.

5 *Well*, normally an adverb, functions as an adjective here.

6 *Elderly* is an adjective with the form of an adverb.

D 1(a), 2(c), 3(d), 4(b); *too* indicates an excess; *rather* often indicates more than is really desirable; *quite* frequently indicates a moderately positive reaction by the speaker.

21 Relative clauses

A 1 (a) Correct.
(b) Incorrect. Commas must be deleted to make sense.
(c) Correct.
(d) Correct.
(e) Incorrect. Commas needed before *which* and *but*.
(f) Correct.
(g) Correct.
(h) Incorrect. Substitute *which* for *that*.
(i) Incorrect. Delete comma.
(j) Correct.

(k) Incorrect. Comma needed before *who*.

(l) Possibly acceptable, but certainly better with *who* substituted for *that*.

2 The commas are so important because they distinguish between a relative clause which **defines** and one which does not.

B 1 A defining relative clause is an essential explanation which makes sense out of an utterance:
Child: The man hit me, mummy. (inadequate information)
Mother: Which man? (seeking essential closer identification)
Child: The one who sometimes comes to tea. (identifying more closely)
Examples from exercise **A** are (b), (c), (d), (g), etc.

2 A non-defining relative clause adds extra, non-essential, information to an utterance. Examples from exercise **A** are (a), (e), (f), (h), etc.

3 Non-defining relative clauses are fairly uncommon in spoken English as they render an utterance somewhat unwieldy. There is a tendency for sentences to be shorter and snappier in spoken English.

C 1 It is possible to omit the *object* pronoun (but not the subject pronoun) in defining relative clauses.

2 Because the relative clause is not so easy to identify in the absence of the relative pronoun. The sense may not be immediately clear.

D The prepositional phrases *in the red dress, on the hill above the village* and *by the door* all have similar force to relative clauses and could be expanded to be relative clauses:

… *who is wearing the red dress* …
… *which is on the hill which is above the village* …
… *which is by the door* …

E The fact that the relative pronoun refers to the whole preceding clause. (There are many languages in which relative pronouns are not used in this way.)

F 1 Subject pronoun *who* wrongly omitted. Learner may not realize that only object relative pronouns can be omitted.

2 Student does not realize that *who* must be used for people and *which* for things.

3 Student does not realize that *who* is the object of *spoke to* and feels the need for an object after the verb. A common mistake among Arabic and Farsi speakers.

4 False analogy (preposition at end) with *That's the house she lives in.*

5 *Whom* should be omitted. Student does not realize it is inappropriate in spoken English.

6 Learner does not realize that *that* cannot always be substituted for *which*, and certainly not in a relative clause referring back to the whole of the previous clause.

G All are **cleft** type sentences in which a clause beginning with *it* or *what* precedes the main clause of the sentence, or in some cases (5 and 6) itself forms the subject of the following verb. In all of the examples a shift of emphasis is achieved.

1 It was Clara … (not someone else!).
2 It could have been Fred … (someone did ring; Fred is a possibility).
3 … and not last Thursday or last Saturday.
4 Emphasis on *Where* would indicate that the questioner once knew but has forgotten.
5 Extra emphasis gained by introductory clause.
6 Whole clause needed here as a subject of sentence.

Compare these less emphatic versions:
1 You saw Clara waiting at the corner.
2 Fred might have rung you up last night.
3 I first felt ill last Friday.
4 Where did you spend the weekend?
5 You get what you see.
6 Your real beliefs are important.

22 Word order

A 1 All of them include inversions of subject and verb (either with or without an auxiliary).
2 (a) Normal interrogative formation – present simple tense.
(b) Normal interrogative formation with modal auxiliary verb.
(c) The position of *only* (at the beginning of the sentence for emphasis) requires inversion of subject and verb in the main clause.
(d) The position of *hardly* at the beginning of the sentence provokes inversion of subject and verb. *Hardly* is one of a group of negative words and expressions (cf also (i)) which require this inversion when used to start a sentence.
(e) A normal tail question (negative question tagged on to a statement).
(f) Here, *Pop* is seen as an example of direct speech, and subject and verb are often inverted afterwards, cf '*Hello,' said John.*
(g) Inversion is normal after demonstrative adverbs *here* and *there*.
(h) Inversion after *so* is normal, though not obligatory. However, it is made more likely in this case because the subject, *all of us*, consists of more than one word.
(i) The negative expression *Under no circumstances* at the beginning of the sentence requires subsequent inversion (cf (d) above).
(j) This is a 'fixed phrase' with the meaning *Let it be so*. The inversion may be influenced by the initial position of *so* (cf (h) above).
(k) Normal inversion after *neither*.
(l) Inversion here adds to the effect of a *live* commentary.
(m) Inversion here replaces an *if* clause.

B Type 1 All of these are examples of inversion after **negative** expressions. The auxiliary *do (does)* is used in each case, as in the interrogative.

Type 2 In these examples, all in the present simple, there is straightforward transposition of subject and verb (for different reasons in each case), without an auxiliary.

C   ✗ *Here my friend comes* (noun subject) would sound strange.
✗ *Here comes she* (pronoun subject) is not possible.
Up into the clear blue sky the bird soared (noun subject) would be possible but less striking.
✗ *Up into the clear blue sky soared it* (pronoun subject) is not possible.
Pronouns do not admit inversion in such utterances.

D   1   *Often* (adverb of frequency) should not usually immediately follow the verb it modifies. The most common correct version would be: *They often go to London.*

   2   *Marvellously* intrudes between the verb and its subject, which should normally not be separated. Corrected version: *My sister plays tennis marvellously.*

   3   The order of the adjectives is unlikely, if not incorrect. Depending on how closely the word *cuddly* defines *teddy*, a more acceptable version would be *a new pink cuddly teddy*.

   4   *Lend* is one of a group of verbs which can take both a direct and an indirect object. If the indirect object is a pronoun and the direct object is a noun, the following word order applies: *Lend me your pen* (or *Lend your pen to me*).
   If both objects are nouns, the order is as follows: *He lent Jim his pen* (or *He lent his pen to Jim*).
   If the direct object is a pronoun and the indirect object a noun, the word order required is: *He lent it to his teacher.*
   So an acceptable version of the example in this exercise would be: *I've lent it to John and his friends.*
   (Most grammar books supply a full list of verbs which can take both direct and indirect objects.)

   5   The adverb *always* rarely starts a sentence. Corrected version: *I always make that mistake.*

   6   Adjective *old* intrudes between the two parts of the noun group *man's coat*. The corrected version *That's an old man's coat* has two possible interpretations. Is it the man or the coat that is old? Reading aloud may help!

   7   Theoretically, the word order is correct here. The speaker has learnt that a negative word at the beginning of a sentence requires subsequent inversion. He has, however, not learnt that such constructions are not appropriate to informal, everyday speech but are reserved for more formal spoken and written styles. Corrected version: *I am not going anywhere this evening.*

1 Common myths and misconceptions about words

1 You cannot stop words from developing new meanings. It is part of the dynamic process of the development of languages. Many words are now used with meanings which are very different from their original meanings. For example, *buxom* used to mean obedient but now it refers to the healthy, attractive appearance of large-breasted women like those in Rubens' paintings.
   In many dictionaries now the primary meaning of *gay* is given as homosexual – for example, in the *Collins Cobuild English Language Dictionary* where the meaning of 'lively and enjoyable to be with' is described as 'slightly more old-fashioned'.

2 This ideal is unattainable as different cultures have different ways of representing the world around them and even have different worlds around them. For example, the Russian word *noga* is usually translated as *leg* even though its referent includes the leg and the foot; a green traffic light is referred to in Japanese as *ao* (literally *blue*); the Lozi word *munyanaka* is translated as *brother* even though it can refer to any related male who is not your father or uncle; and the French word *le pain* refers to something which looks and tastes very different from the referent of its translation *bread*. Also words are often borrowed from a language but are then used with a broader reference than in the original language. Thus *sukejuuru* in Japanese refers to both a formal schedule and an informal intention and *koosu* in Japanese refers to both a course for a race and a path or route for walking.

3 This is also unattainable for the same reasons given in 2 above. Thus the translation of *He's bought a dog* in Chinese or Arabic would be interpreted in different ways from in the original because of the different attitudes towards the function of dogs in the cultures represented by these languages. This would probably be true also of *They've killed a whale* translated into Japanese or Norwegian.

4 Using borrowed words can cause confusion if they are not in common use (eg *simpático*) and annoyance if a perfectly adequate word already exists (eg *le weekend*). But all languages borrow words to cover meanings they do not have a native word for. *Yacht, amok* and *bureau* are examples of English words borrowed from other languages.

5 It is not possible to say that one word is the correct one to use to refer to a particular referent. The best word to use is the one most efficient in the circumstances. Thus if there is only one thing on the table it would be much more sensible to ask someone helping you to pass the *thing on the table* or the *piece of wood* than the *joist*. However if you are ordering things from a specialist carpenter suppliers you are more likely to use the term *joist*. In the same way when watching a game of bowls in the park you would say to someone who has never seen a game before, *She bowled that one well* but would say, *Great wood!* to a bowls enthusiast.

6 Slang is normally most appropriate when talking to someone you know who

Commentary

shares group membership with you (eg a fellow teenage rap or indie enthusiast) but it would also be completely acceptable in a letter to a friend, in a newsletter of a particular association or group, (eg a school rugby club) or in an advertisement aimed at a particular group of enthusiasts (eg for a pop concert).

7 What are considered to be taboo topics and words varies from culture to culture. Thus in England we often find euphemisms when referring to the toilet, to sex and to death (eg *the little boys' room, lovemaking* and *passed away*) but in other cultures much more explicit words are used without embarrassment in public. Thus it is quite possible that you might be asked at a dinner party in Indonesia, *Which condoms do you use?* but you would never be asked, *What do you think of communism?*

8 Some people seem to be able to build up their active and passive vocabularies through conscious learning of definitions and translations but most people seem to benefit more from experiencing lexical items being used for real communication in the language being learned. Although learning definitions and translations can help you when you have time to think (eg when reading or writing) it cannot really help very much when you need to understand or produce words in spontaneous conversation. And even if it did it could cause you to make errors because of differences of reference and implication between translation equivalents.

2 Word fields and lexical relationships

A (a) This is one possible answer: 1; 2; 3, 5; 4; 6, 7; 8, 10, 11, 12; 9.

(b) There is no definite answer to this question – only opinions. It could be argued that the core meaning includes doing something in a small space or restricted area.

(c) The important conclusion is that *pick* has many meanings and that some of them would not be relevant to learners of an intermediate level (eg as in sentences 2, 4, 5, 8, 9, 11 and 12). In addition, teaching a learner all the different meanings of *pick* at the same time would inevitably lead to confusion and to ineffective learning.

If is useful to decide that there are many different words which are spelled and pronounced *pick* and to teach only those which are likely to be useful to the learner. *Pick up*, as in sentence 1, is common and useful, as is *pick* in sentence 3 and *pick up* in sentence 7.

There is no one correct answer to the question of which *picks* to teach to an intermediate group; the important thing is that the teacher is selective and teaches only those *picks* which the learners should know.

In order to avoid the possibility of confusion it is better to teach the different selected *picks* at different times.

Most of the *pick* sentences in **A** would not be good teaching examples as in most cases the sentences do not provide very much information about the meanings of *pick* (eg sentences 2 and 11). It is useful to exemplify new vocabulary items in contexts which help the learner to appreciate the meaning of the new item.

eg *Pick that glass up off the floor and put it on the table before somebody stands on it.*

(d) Instead of referring the student to a dictionary the teacher could have referred him/her to the passage. The student's question makes it obvious that he/she does not realize that the item he/she does not know the meaning of is *pick up* and not *pick*. The dictionary will give many meanings of *pick* and the student will have great difficulty in finding the one relevant to the passage. In addition it is quite likely that he/she will not understand the definition even if a relevant one is found.

Dictionaries can be an aid to vocabulary acquisition but only when the students have been taught how to use them and only if the students use them to check deductions they have made after analysing the form of the words and the contexts in which they have met them.

The teacher who persistently tells students to look words up in their dictionaries is encouraging the sort of painful intensive reading which consists of looking up every unfamiliar word regardless of its usefulness to the learner or its significance in the text.

(e) Students should be discouraged from asking such questions and encouraged instead to pay more attention to the overall meaning of the text than to the exact meaning of every vocabulary item in it.

The question is best answered by saying that *pick* has many meanings and that the student should examine the passage he/she is reading to try to discover clues to the particular meaning of *pick* in the passage. The teacher should lead the student to discover that he/she is looking for the meaning of *pick up* in the text and to examine the previous and subsequent sentences for clues (such as the fact that the speaker has a car and that the two are going to travel in it together).

(f) Only one of the definitions is relevant to the student's problem. The others are not only irrelevant but are meanings which are unlikely to be useful to an intermediate student even if he manages to learn them all without confusion. Learning definitions does not magically bestow on the learner the ability to understand the word in context and does nothing at all to help use it accurately and appropriately.

A learner could write five correct, *safe* sentences which tell the teacher nothing about the learner's ability to understand or use the item, eg *Have you ever been to a port?* or *I can see a port.*

B 1 The words in italics in each pair have the same referent (ie they refer to the same thing). Thus *slim* and *skinny* refer to the same physical characteristic of the same girl. However in each pair the words might have the same referent but they do not have exactly the same meaning. In each pair the two speakers have different attitudes to the same thing. Thus in (a) the first speaker does not like what William has become whereas the second speaker does; in (b) the first speaker finds Alice attractive whereas the second does not.

We can say that in each pair the words have the same referent but that they have different implied meanings.

2 (a) The implied meanings of the words should be taught as well as their referents.

(b) We should be very careful to distinguish between two items which are similar (but different) in meaning.

(c) It can be useful to introduce a new item by relating it to a similar item which is familiar to the learners providing that attention is focused on both the similarities and the differences.

C 1 (a) *picture*   (b) *shoes*   (c) *pen*   (d) *meat*   (e) *seat* . . . etc.

2 The replacements are all more general than the words in italics. They could refer to many different types (eg *picture* – photo, drawing, painting, portrait, sketch, etc).

3 (a) When teaching beginners it is important to select items which have a high coverage; that is, words which can be used by the beginner instead of other words. Thus *seat* can be used instead of *chair, sofa, bench*, etc and should thus be taught before them.

(b) A word with high coverage is usually the most general item in a 'family'. Thus *picture* is the most general item in the family which contains *photo, painting, drawing*, etc. Advanced learners should be able to understand and use many of the particular items as well as the general item in each of the common word families in English.

When teaching a particular item from a family it is important to focus attention not only on its membership of the family but also on how it is different from the general item and from the other particular items in the family which have already been taught. Thus when teaching *bench* it is important to show that it is a particular type of *seat* and that the words cannot always be used interchangeably and to show how a *bench* is different from a *chair* and a *sofa*.

D 1 In all the sentences the speaker has used a word which has a meaning which is close to the one he wants to communicate but which for various reasons is not appropriate. Thus in (a) the writer has used *fracture* to mean *break* because he is unaware that *fracture* can only refer to the breaking of particular types of things (mainly bones). In (d) the writer has used *feeble* to mean *weak* because he is unaware that *feeble* is normally only used to refer to animate things (mainly people) which are weak.

Almost certainly the writer has made these errors because he has learned a new word as a synonym of one he already knows either as a result of consulting a dictionary, of incompletely deducing the meaning of a new word or of being taught that the new word = the known word. Thus the writer has learned that *manufacture* = *make* but has not learned that the two words are not always interchangeable because *manufacture* can normally only be used when things are made in bulk and made to be sold.

2 It is dangerous to teach or to imply that two words are synonyms (ie that their meanings are exactly the same).

It is important to teach when an item cannot be used as well as when it can be used. One way of achieving this is to teach the item together with known words which it is frequently used with (eg *eject from/meeting*) and then to give examples of the types of words it cannot be used with (eg ✗ *pierce/window*).

Another way is to demonstrate the difference between the two related words (eg by contrasting pictures of people walking and people marching, and by asking questions about their purposes).

E 1 The definitions consist only of equivalent words; they include no information about when it is appropriate to use the word being defined instead of its equivalent. For example, there is no information about when it would be appropriate to use *mate* (eg in informal conversation) and when it would not (eg in a formal interview).

2 The learner would probably think that the words were interchangeable and use those with restricted appropriacy (ie those being defined) in situations in which their use would be inappropriate (eg a worker addressing a letter requesting a rise to *The Boss*; someone starting a report, *Ten guys were selected for training*).

3 One-word definitions are often dangerous because they give the impression that the two words are interchangeable (ie that one can always be used instead of the other).

It is important to teach when it is appropriate to use an item and also to teach when it is not appropriate to use an item.

F 1 (a) Once two opposites have been taught it is often useful to indicate on a sloping line the relative positions of the items used to refer to degrees in between the opposites. This is particularly useful for example for showing that *quite good* is less than *good*.
(b) Degrees in between opposites can be referred to by *either* (i) adding another word to one of the opposites (eg *quite hot*) *or* (ii) using a different item (eg *warm*). It is usually easier to teach (i) first and then later to teach (ii).

2 The same items can appear on two different lines of opposition. Thus *good* can appear on a line of ability as well as on a line of virtue. It is important that the learner does not assume that the other items can appear on both lines, or he might, for example, use *poor* as an equivalent to *bad* on the line of virtue.

G 1 In most contexts *reach* and *arrive* can have the same meaning and are equally acceptable. However, *reach = get in touch with* cannot be replaced by *arrive* and *reach out = stretch out* cannot be replaced by *arrive out*. *Reach* must always be followed by an object whereas *arrive* need not be. *Reach* cannot be used with *back* whereas *arrive* can. *Arrive* must be followed by *at* when its object noun is preceded by an article whereas *reach* is never followed by *at*.
Brave and *courageous* appear to be interchangeable. However, whereas in many contexts *courage* seems to be able to replace *bravery*, *bravery* only seems to be able to replace *courage* when physical actions rather than mental actions are being referred to. In certain fixed phrases *bravery* can never be used instead of *courage*. There is no verb *to courage* corresponding to the verb *to brave*.
Put up and *accommodate* seem to communicate the same meaning but *accommodate* is not normally used in informal conversation.

2 To be totally interchangeable two words must be capable of always substituting for each other without changing the grammar, the meaning or the acceptability of the utterance.

3 It is sometimes useful to introduce a new item by relating it to a similar item which is already known. However, it is very important to point out any potential differences in meaning, grammar or acceptability and learners should never be left with the impression that word A = word B (except for the few pairs which are totally interchangeable). It is also important to show that even if two words are apparently interchangeable their related forms might not be (eg *brave* v *courageous*; *bravery* v *courage*).

3 Factors in the teaching of vocabulary

A 1 It is important to realize that two words which are considered to be opposites will rarely be capable of a relationship of opposition in all conceivable contexts. If two words are introduced as opposites or if a new word is introduced as the opposite of a known word it is important to show when the two words are not opposites as well as when they are.

2 There is some point in teaching all these pairs together providing that initially the relationship of opposition is demonstrated in appropriate contexts, that the students never learn that word A = the opposite of word B and that eventually contexts are used to show when the two words are not opposites.

B 1 (a) and (b) are useless teaching examples as in both cases the context gives no clue to the meaning of *amazed*. In (c) *found out* gives some sort of clue to the meaning of *amazed* but it is not a very informative teaching example. (d) is a good teaching example as it contains a lot of information to help the learner work out the meaning of *amazed*. (e) gives clues to the unexpected aspect of *amazed* but is not a very good teaching example as it could give the misleading impression that *amazed* is always used to refer to unpleasant surprises (cf (d)).

2 Such examples should be as informative as possible and ideally should enable the learner to accurately deduce the meaning of a word which is totally new to him.

C 1 The sentences say very little about the ability of the students to use *swept* as all the sentences are *safe* sentences which accurately imitate a model but do not contain any information which enables you to decide whether the students know why or how you sweep a carpet.

2 Asking students to write sentences using a particular word is basically a waste of time as very often correct sentences are produced which reveal nothing about the students' ability to understand and use the word. However, if such an exercise is set and safe answers are produced the teacher can probe by asking such questions as *Why did she sweep it?* and *What did she sweep it with?*

D 1 (a) *nibbit* = biscuit (or possibly cake)
Clues:
in your pocket – therefore small and probably wrapped.
in case I was hungry – therefore edible and probably more substantial than a sweet.
prefer the ones with chocolate on.
That's probably why I didn't eat it.
(b) *slinned* = cleaned
Clues:
took your coat to be – not done at home therefore probably done in a shop.
I hope they get all the stains out this time – therefore definitely not *mended* or *altered* and almost certainly *cleaned* rather than *washed* (not normally done in shops or to coats anyway).
2 *ding* = slap
Clues:
ding him – therefore done to someone.

hard – therefore physical.
He ... naughty – therefore a boy.
hurt – confirms physical.
hand – therefore not cane, ruler or fist.
on his leg – therefore not *punch*.
soon get over it – therefore not serious.

3 (a) *glogget* = deckchair or folding chair
Clues:
sitting in the garden.
didn't want it to get wet.
folded it up.
put it in the garage.
with the other garden seats.
(b) *unseddy* = untidy
Clues:
I was furious
I'd told the kids to put all their toys in the trunk to keep the garage seddy.
there were toys all over the garage floor.

Learners can be taught to try to deduce the meaning of unfamiliar items from an analysis of the context.

E 1 and 2 Various answers are possible. Our answers were:

(a) get something back (verb)
(b) a book with a card cover (adjective or noun)
(c) having too much of something (noun)
(d) below the moon (adjective)
(e) twice a day (adjective or adverb)
(f) like a punk (adverb)
(g) think afterwards (verb) *or* the period after thinking (noun)
(h) make impossible (verb)
(i) recommend that something does not happen *or* withdraw a recommendation (both verb)
(j) good at attending (adjective)

3 It is useful to teach students the meanings of common roots (eg *possib*) and prefixes (eg *post-*) and about how prefixes modify the meaning of roots. It is also useful to teach the grammatical and semantic functions of common suffixes (eg *-ate*).
Often a learner can work out the meaning of an unfamiliar word by examining the form and the context of the word.

4 It is a good idea to warn students that there are exceptions and that they should always check their guesses against information in the context.

F 1 ? It was sensational to hear.
? It was amazing to eat.
✗ It was superlative to eat/watch/hear/drive.
✗ It was brilliant to eat/hear/drive.

2 All the words in column 2 could be used interchangeably in such a sentences as *It was a(n) — film.* However they are not always interchangeable. For instance

101

it seems that *brilliant* when used in the pattern *It was + adjective + infinitive* is restricted to reference to *performances* and that *superlative* cannot be used in this pattern at all. It also seems that some of the adjectives in column 2 simply mean *very good* (ie *marvellous, superb* and *wonderful*) while others can sometimes mean *very good* but can also have other meanings (eg *amazing* can mean *very good* or *very surprising*).

3 It is dangerous to assume that certain words are always interchangeable because they are interchangeable in a particular type of context.

It can be useful to teach words in families providing that the grammatical and semantic sub-groupings are made evident.

G 2 The words belong to the same family but are by no means interchangeable. Sub-groups can be formed on the basis of features of meaning. Thus sub-group A1 might consist of *bought, purchased, hired, rented, borrowed, leased* and *acquired* while sub-group A2 consisted of *loaned, let, rented out, sold, leased* and *lent*. A1 involves *movement towards* the subject. A2 involves *movement away* from the subject. Another sub-grouping could be B1 *(bought, purchased, hired, rented, rented out, sold, leased, let)*, B2 *(borrowed, lent)* and B3 *(acquired, loaned)*. B1 *includes* the payment of money, B2 *excludes* the payment of money, and B3 could either include or exclude the payment of money.

Yet another sub-grouping could be C1 *(purchased, leased; acquired, loaned)* and C2 (all other items). The items in C1 are restricted in use in that they are normally only used in formal (and usually business) situations whereas the items in C2 are not restricted in this way.

The words also differ in collocation (ie the words they can acceptably be used with). Thus *leased* is restricted in collocation to *house* and *business* and words like them. *Rented* can collocate with *house, car, business, tent, television* and words like them (ie words which refer to things you pay money for the continuous use of) and *hired* can collocate with such words as *house, car, business, tent, maid, television* and *picture* (ie words referring to things or people you can pay to use for a short time). Another example of restricted collocation is the fact that *lent* cannot normally be followed immediately by *a* (eg ✗ *I've lent a car*) while *acquired* cannot normally be followed immediately by *my* when it is preceded by the present perfect (eg ✗ *I've acquired my business*). *Lent* could be said to belong to sub-group D1 and *acquired* to D2.

H This is a useful exercise for teaching the collocations of items in a *family* and thus for helping to teach the differences in meaning and use between the items.

It is important to realize that this exercise is only one stage in teaching learners to use the items accurately and appropriately as knowledge does not automatically lead to ability to use.

4 Phrasal and prepositional verbs

A Category one (verb + preposition): 4, 5, 7, 8 (prepositional verbs)
Category two (verb + adverb): 1, 2, 3, 6 (phrasal verbs)

B Each verb is followed by an adverbial particle and then a preposition.

C 1 He'll have to be spoken *to* firmly (*to* is unstressed).
    2 This work will have to be put *aside* (*aside* is stressed).
    3 Three of the crew cannot be accounted *for* (*for* is unstressed).
    4 The house was cleaned *up* after the party (*up* is stressed).
    5 This form has been filled *in* (*in* is stressed).
    6 A lot of ships have been laid *up* in the south-west of England (*up* is stressed).
    7 The steelworks have been shut *down* (*down* is stressed).
    8 This record has been worn *out* (*out* is stressed).

Foreign learners often find it difficult to distinguish between phrasal and prepositional verbs. This provides a useful test. Phrasal verbs (with adverb particles) carry stress on the adverb in the passive, and the adverb can be separated from the verb by its object – this applies to 2, 4, 5, 6, 7, 8 above. Prepositional verbs cannot be *split* and the preposition is unstressed in passive sentences. This applies to 1 and 3.

D 1 *catch on* means understand; not deducible from its parts.
    2 *answer back* – the meaning can be deduced straightforwardly from the parts.
    3 *gone off* – idiomatic meaning; not directly deducible.
    4 *let down* – the meaning can be deduced from the parts.
    5 *let down* – idiomatic meaning; not directly deducible.
    6 *lay in* – idiomatic meaning; not directly deducible.
    7 *run down* – idiomatic meaning; not directly deducible.
    8 *put out* – idiomatic meaning; not directly deducible.
    9 *stand up* – the meaning can be deduced from the parts.
   10 *ran away* – the meaning can be deduced from the parts.
   11 *knock off* – idiomatic meaning; not directly deducible.
   12 *brush up* – idiomatic meaning; not directly deducible.

E The exercise asks for phrasal verb synonyms for the Latin-based words in the exercise. It would be more useful if it gave some indication of when the Latinate equivalents are more appropriate (phrasal verbs tend to occur more in *informal* speech and writing). No reason is given for the substitution as an exercise. The verbs required are:

1	taken out	6	left out
2	bought up	7	gave (him) away
3	looks like	8	get away
4	put off	9	died out
5	running (your brother) down	10	cut down

NB Phrasal and prepositional verbs cause foreign learners a lot of difficulty, for reasons demonstrated in these exercises. They are best dealt with as items of vocabulary each time they appear, and learners should be encouraged to note down examples each time they meet a new verb of this type. R. A. Close in *A Reference Grammar for Students of English* (Longman) offers a very full treatment of the subject, with useful categorization, and there is a more exhaustive treatment in A.P. Cowie and R. Mackin (1993) *The Oxford Dictionary of English Idioms* which is devoted to phrasal and prepositional verbs.

The main structural teaching point is to give learners criteria for distinguishing between the types (see **B** and **C** above) so that they can handle the syntax.

Unit 4 **Cohesion**

A 1 Because it is not clear what the pronouns refer to. For example, what is *it* and who is *him* in sentence (a)?

2 *Either* the pronouns rewritten as nouns,
or other utterances from the same conversations containing nouns referred to by the pronouns, eg (a) *What's Bill's medicine doing here? Have you given it to him yet?*
or information about the situations in which the utterances were made, eg (d) *Two children are watching a film. They look bored. Mary points to the children and says, 'Have they seen it before?'*

3 Obviously there are many possible answers to this question. One possibility is:
   (a) Have you given your homework to the teacher yet?
   (b) Are we seeing Bill and Mary again tonight?
   (c) Did you buy your car from Joe Flynn?
   (d) Have your children seen the film before?
   (e) If I see Fred with Sophia again I'll tell you.
   (f) Why did your daughter get angry?
       – Her husband was very drunk.
   (g) Sheila's dress is very beautiful.

4 If the nouns had not been recently referred to and if there was nothing in the situation which made it clear what or who was being referred to, eg (c) *Two men were sitting in a pub discussing a secondhand radio which one of them had bought from a local dealer. One of the men asked, 'Did you buy your car from Joe Flynn?' because he wanted to confirm that this was true before going on to compare the two secondhand dealers.*

5 If the previous utterance(s) or something in the situation had made it absolutely clear what or who was being referred to, eg (g) *I get so envious of Sarah. My face is ugly. Look. Hers is beautiful.*

6 Yes. For example, if the noun had already been mentioned by the speaker and the situation made it perfectly clear what was being referred to, eg (d) ✗ *Look at the children. The children seem bored by this film. Have the children seen this film before?*

7 They are used to refer to people and things that have already been mentioned or are present in the situation. They help to avoid repeating expressions and stating the obvious and therefore contribute to the economy of utterances.

8 Because they refer to people who are present in the situation and therefore who do not need to be identified.
They refer to participants in the conversation whereas the other pronouns usually refer to non-participants in the conversation and to people and things which are being identified either by reference back to what has been said or by *pointing* to them in the situation.

9 *her* is used to refer to a person whereas *hers* is used to refer to both the person and to something that belongs to her.

B 1 (a) *A* has wrongly assumed that *B* will know the place referred to by *there*.

          (b) *A* has wrongly assumed that *B* will know the time referred to by *then*.

          (c) *A* has wrongly assumed that *B* will know the things referred to by *those*.

          (d) *A* has wrongly assumed that *B* will know the thing referred to by *that*.

    2 They refer to places, times or things which have previously been mentioned or which have been specified by the situation. They help to avoid repetition and to achieve economy.

    3 *they, him, then, there. A* was right in assuming that *B* would perceive their referents (ie what they refer to) as a result of relating to previous mention or from pointers in the situation.

    4 (a) *A:* Are they going there again?

              B: Who?

          (b) I saw him then.

              Who?

          (c) I'm doing those then.

              When?

          (d) Did you buy that there?

              Where?

C 1 Because the words with potential for breakdown in communication (ie *I, you, this, these, yours, here, now*) refer to referents present in the situation.

    2 All the words refer to referents which have previously been mentioned or are *pointed to* in the situation. However those in (a) refer to referents present and close in the situation whereas those in (b) refer to referents either distant from the speaker or not present in the situation at all.

D 1 *B*'s *that* refers back to the vase. *A*'s *that* refers back to the breaking of the vase.

    2 *A*'s *this* refers back to the house. *B*'s *this* refers to what they are doing (ie to the situation).

E 1 (a) Could mean that the books were not the same as the two books previously referred to whereas (b) could mean that the books were different from each other.

          In (a) *different* refers you to previous utterances or to features of the situation to complete a contrast whereas in (b) *different* acts as an adjective establishing a contrast between the two books mentioned in the utterance.

    2 (a) *A:* No! I don't mean new clothes. I mean different clothes. I don't want to get these dirty.

          (b) *Other* warns you to refer to the situation and to previous utterances to help you decide whether it is being used with its function of addition or its function of replacement.

    3 (a) *More* could refer back to a referent made clear by previous utterances or by the situation (eg *more potatoes*) or it could be part of an expression indicating that the speaker thinks greater efforts are needed.

          (b) *A* realizes that more people than expected have turned up to a function and says to *B We haven't done enough sandwiches. We'll have to do more.*

          A is talking to *B* about a student who is not performing well and says, *We haven't done enough to help him. We'll have to do more.*

F 1 They are all acting as substitutes for elements in previous utterances (eg in (a) *one* is acting as a substitute for *cooker*).

   2 (a), (e), (g) act as substitutes for nouns;
      (b), (d) as substitutes for verbs;
      (c), (f) as substitutes for clauses; and
      (h), (i) as substitutes for possessive pronoun plus noun.

G 1 In all the utterances something has been omitted (eg *bought* in (a)).

   2 Group one (b, c, d, g) – nouns omitted.
      Group two (a, e, f, h, i) – verbs omitted.

   3 (a) Instead of repeating the same main verb in adjacent clauses or sentences you can often omit it in the second utterance.
      (b) Instead of repeating the same auxiliary verbs in adjacent clauses or sentences you can often omit them (provided the main verbs are different and are included in the utterance).
      (c) Instead of repeating the same subject in adjacent clauses or sentences you can often omit the subject in the second utterance.
      (d) Instead of repeating the same object in adjacent clauses or sentences you can often omit the object in the second utterance.

H 3 All the sentences could indicate an equal liking for football and rugby but sentences (c), (d), (e), (f), and (i) could indicate a preference for football whereas sentences h and j could indicate a preference for rugby. The actual interpretation would depend on the intonation of the speaker, the previous utterances and features of the situation.

   4 Type 1: *and.* Joins two clauses within the same sentence; must come in between them.
      Type 2: *as well as*; *in addition to.* Joins two clauses within the same sentence; can come at the beginning of the first clause or in between the first and second.
      Type 3: *also*; *in addition.* Joins two sentences together.

   5 (k), (l), (m) and (p) focus attention on the contrast between the expected and the actual performance of the car. (n) and (o) focus attention on the fine performance of the car and then add the regrettable fact that it is old.

   6 Type 1: *but*
      Type 2: *although*
      Type 3: *however*

I 2 Type 1: *and*; *also*
      Type 2: *at the same time*; *then*; *so*; *as well as*
      Type 3: *at the same time*; *then*; *and all the other items in the list*

   3

Exemplification	Sequence	Reason	Result	Purpose	Comparison
for instance	first	for this reason	as a result	for this purpose	in the same way
for example	finally	in that case	because of this	with this in mind	likewise
thus		then	thus		similarly
		so	consequently		
		on account of this	therefore		
		therefore	then		
			so		

Addition	Contrast	Correction	Dismissal	Reinforcement	Time
and also	nevertheless	rather	anyhow	moreover	meanwhile
besides	even so	at least		in fact	at the same time
as well as	despite this	instead		as a matter of fact	previously
	however	on the other hand		in any case	finally
	on the other hand			besides	
	on the contrary			furthermore	

NB Some of the items could also belong to other categories, eg *instead* could belong to *Replacement*.

4 Some of the differences are:
   (a) Some of the expressions are used mainly in formal situations or in writing, eg *on account of this*; *for this purpose*; *thus*; *likewise*; *similarly*; *furthermore*.
   (b) Some of the categories could be subdivided, eg

   Contrast

Concession	Balance	Opposition
nevertheless	on the other hand	on the contrary
even so		
despite this		
however		

   (c) Some of the expressions are restricted as regards the linguistic environment they can be used in, eg *as a matter of fact* is normally used to reinforce a point following or in anticipation of an objection or challenge; *in that case* cannot be used with past reference.

J 1 *Meanwhile* is normally used to indicate a connection in time and in type between two events. Here it is only used to indicate a connection in time as a sinking and a heatwave are not connected in type.
   2 *Nevertheless* suggests that something has just been referred to that might prevent enjoyment whereas the opposite is true.
   3 *Anyhow* is not normally used to indicate resignation or concession; in this sentence it has been wrongly used instead of *however* or possibly *anyway*.
   4 *On the contrary* is wrongly used. It is normally used to indicate contradiction in utterances, eg *Many people think that I'm going to resign. On the contrary, I'm going to work harder than ever before for the committee.*
      In sentence 4 jazz and folk music are not opposites.
   5 *In that case* is wrongly used with past reference. It is normally only used with future reference, eg *A: It's just started to rain.*
      B: In that case we'd better take our coats after all.

K

1 plan; thing to do	3 stuff	5 thing	7 woman
2 place	4 idea	6 boy; lad	8 creature

All these are lexical substitutes used to represent items previously identified. They avoid repetition and in many cases indicate that the speaker has a negative attitude towards the referent, eg instead of *Put it away in that cupboard*, the expression used is *Put the thing away in that cupboard*. In many of the sentences much stronger *negative* words could have been used than the ones chosen (eg *brat*, *rascal* in 6).

M It is important to teach the ways in which utterances are linked in English. If we do not our learners might understand the meaning of an utterance but not appreciate how it is connected with previous and subsequent utterances and they might be able to produce isolated utterances but not be able to produce continuous discourse.

It is important that the teacher understands the ways in which English achieves cohesion (ie the ways it uses to link various types of utterances) and makes use of this understanding in the planning of teaching and practice material. It is particularly important that such material gives the learners the opportunity to respond to, participate in and produce extended and continuous discourse.

A

Type	Purpose
1 *A:* interrogative	offer
B: declarative	declining offer
A: declarative	repeating and strengthening offer
B: declarative (negative)	explaining the declining of the offer
2 *A:* declarative + interrogative	seeking confirmation
B: declarative	confirming
A: declarative	statement of consequent action
B: interrogative	polite request
3 *A:* declarative	statement of fact + criticism and indication of worry
B: imperative + declarative	reassurance
A: declarative	criticism + indication of worry
B: interrogative	criticism + indication of annoyance

NB Other interpretations are possible (eg 2 *A:* = *incentive to action*) as information about the relationship between the speakers, the setting of the dialogue, the shared knowledge of the speakers and the intonation, pace and volume of the utterances is needed before a completely objective analysis can be attempted.

B   1   (a) *A* is reminding *B* that he is supposed to ring somebody at seven.
(b) A wife is suggesting to her husband that he should cut the grass in their garden, as they are expecting visitors. The husband does not want to do it and reminds her that he is meeting someone soon and that he has been late for appointments with this person for the last two weeks.
(c) A boy is driving his girlfriend home and suggests that they should stop for a drink at a pub. She is reluctant to stop and he tries to persuade her by suggesting that they might meet her friend.
(d) A boy answers the phone and is mistaken for his brother. He tells the caller that his brother has left and suggests where he might be.

NB There are of course numerous other situations in which the exchanges would make sense.

2

Type	Purpose
(b) *A:* declarative	getting somebody to do something
B: declarative	avoiding doing something
This pattern is repeated twice.	
(c) *A:* interrogative	suggestion
B: declarative	expressing reluctance
A: declarative + interrogative	as *A* above
B: declarative	as *B* above
A: declarative + interrogative	persuasion
B: declarative	indicating non-acceptance of suggestion by *A*

(d) *A:* declarative   greeting
     B: interrogative   seeking confirmation
     A: declarative   statement of information
     B: declarative   statement of information + identification
     A: interrogative   expression of surprise + annoyance
     B: imperative   suggestion

NB Other answers are of course possible.

3 (a) It is important to make sure that the learner is not misled into thinking that declarative = statement, interrogative = question and imperative = command.
(b) The learner should be taught to participate in conversations in which the participants share knowledge and experience and therefore do not make the reference and purpose of every utterance explicit.
(c) The learner should be taught how to achieve his or her purpose effectively through language (eg persuade someone to do something; turn down an invitation without giving offence).
(d) Teaching the form and function of structures is not enough. We must also teach how to use them to achieve the purpose of an utterance (eg *My mother will be worried: will be* = prediction, but the whole utterance = reluctance to follow suggestion).
(e) Learners should not be forced to use *full sentences* in dialogue practice unless the situation requires it.

C 1 (a) Advice
     (b) Warning
     (c) Command
     (d) Appeal
     (e) Instruction.

2 *Command*
    (a) *A* in authority over *B*
    (b) *B* accepts authority of *A*
    (c) *A* wants *B* to do something
    (d) *B* capable of doing what *A* wants.

Advice
    (a) *B* in need of help
    (b) *A* accepts that *B* needs help
    (c) *A* in position to help
    (d) *B* accepts that *A* in position to help
    (e) *A* does not intend to do anything but intends *B* to do something.

Appeal
    (a) *A* in great need of help
    (b) help previously asked for
    (c) *B* in position to help *A*.

Instruction
    (a) *A* has greater knowledge, expertise or experience than *B*
    (b) *B* accepts (a)
    (c) *B* needs *A* to say what to do.

Warning

(a) *B* in danger

(b) *A* informing *B* of danger

(c) *B* capable of averting danger

(d) *A* knows how *B* can avert danger.

3 Listing conditions as above can help the teacher to devise situations which will help the learner to appreciate the difference between similar potential functions of the same utterance (eg teacher–pupil in science laboratory for *instruction* and father–young son at home for *command*).

D 1 Criticism through prediction of consequences.

2 Exemplification to reinforce criticism.

3 *all industries should be nationalized* and *let us encourage private enterprise.*

4 When private enterprise has been encouraged?

5 To link *prosperity* to *initiative* as its consequence.

6 (a) Criticism

(b) Prediction

(c) Exemplification

(d) Exemplification

(e) Refutation

(f) Suggestion

(g) Reinforcement of suggestion.

E 1 *No tapes for the winter term.* Because the *answer* refers to tapes.

2 The lack of money as a result of the spending of the budget.

3 *We have a problem,* and *I think I've got an answer.*

4 The use of *that* in *that spare set of 'Mullens'*, implies that the addressee is aware of these books and is therefore working at the school. The *of course* in, *That means of course no tapes* also suggests that the addressee works at the school and therefore that the *we* includes the addressee.

5 Books. Because of *set* and because *'Mullens'* is in inverted commas.

6 It is important to teach how to detect and make links between consecutive and between separated utterances.

F 1 *Furthermore* is normally used to introduce an additional point which reinforces the similar ones already made. In this text it does not seem to have any such semantic function.

2 There is no logical link between sentences 3 and 4 because of the differences in tense.

3 *Another factor* does not logically link its utterance to any previous utterance. Another factor in what?

4 *Especially* does not logically link its utterance to the previous one.

5 Does sentence 6 refer to the electrification of motor vehicles?

6 *However* does not logically link its utterance to the previous one.

7 *As a result* does not logically link its utterance to the previous one.

8 There are no grammatical or vocabulary errors in these two paragraphs but the writer's inability to link his utterances logically makes them very difficult to understand.

Commentary

G Cohesion involves indicating the *connection* between *consecutive* or *related* utterances. If a text is cohesive you can see by *looking* at the text how one utterance is *related* to a *previous* or *subsequent* utterance.

Coherence is the *linking* together of *consecutive* or *related* utterances according to the *functions* of the utterances. Thus an invitation followed by an *acceptance* would be *coherent* whereas an invitation followed by an anecdote probably would not be *coherent*.

Example 1 could be *coherent* because it could consist of a generalization followed by an example and a consequence. But it is not *cohesive* because there is no *indicated connection* between the two utterances.

Example 2 is *cohesive* because the two utterances are connected by the repetition of *London*. But it is not *coherent* because there is no apparent connection between the function of the question and the function of the reply.

Unit 6 **Errors**

1 Some myths and misconceptions about errors

1 Good language learners try to use the language they are learning as much as possible and therefore they make many mistakes. Poor language learners often try to avoid using the language and often only produce short simple utterances when they are required to speak.

2 If a learner produces a language incorrectly it is usually either evidence of an error resulting from faulty internalization or of a mistake caused by such performance factors as tiredness, tension or pressure of time. Errors are consistent and often are indicative of a stage in acquisition rather than of learning something wrongly. Thus a learner who consistently adds *-ed* to irregular verbs to form the simple past (eg *goed*) has probably internalized a valid generalization about the formation of the simple past but has not yet acquired the exceptions (ie has overgeneralized). Mistakes are inconsistent and are made by very advanced learners and even by native speakers. If a learner usually forms the past simple of irregular verbs correctly but just occasionally gets one wrong when very nervous or when trying to express complex content, it does not mean that he/she has learned the simple past incorrectly.

3 Language acquisition does not result from memorization. You can memorize a rule over and over again but it will not help you to produce correct English in spontaneous speech unless you have had sufficient experience of the rule being applied in authentic communication.

4 Learners should not be made to feel guilty or inadequate because they have made an error. If they have to correct every error they make, they feel they are being punished rather than helped and they often become negative about the language they are learning and resentful of the teacher. They lose confidence and motivation and try to avoid using the language that is causing them so much pain.

In all the research into second language acquisition there is no evidence that frequent correction is at all valuable to the learner. But there is considerable evidence that teacher patience and encouragement plus meaningful exposure to the language in use can help the learner to eventually get it right.

5 Many errors are developmental and do not benefit very much from correction. Just like the child learning a first language, the learner of a foreign language goes through the stages of acquisition in which his production of language gradually becomes more correct as internal generalizations are refined from information gained from using the language for communication. However, some errors which are not part of the developmental process (eg those caused by interference from the first language or from mislearning) can eventually be remedied by constructive feedback from the teacher. This is particularly true of such errors made in written English, as usually when writing the learner has time to think about advice given by the teacher.

6 Many language acquisition researchers believe that very few grammatical errors are caused by interference from the first language and that contrasting

grammars of the two languages only confuses the learners. However it does seem that some lexical errors and many pronunciation errors are influenced by the first language and that when such errors are made language contrasts can help in the remedial process.

2   Learners' errors

A   1   (a) *fisherman*
  – False analogy with *baker, farmer,* etc.
  – Overgeneralization that in English agent nouns are formed by adding *-er* to the simple form of the verb.

   (b) *can see*
  – Overgeneralization that the present continuous is always used when reference is being made to a continuous action in the present.
  – Overteaching/overlearning of the present continuous as a result of intensive drilling of the tense in association with *now* situations.
  – Chronology, ie the tense was the first learned and is now dominant.

   (c) *likes*
  – Overgeneralization that the present simple has the same form as the infinitive.
  – Perception of the redundancy of the *s* (ie it is not essential for effective communication).

   (d) *lives*
  – Failure to discriminate between the sound /i/ (in *lives*) and /i:/ (in *leaves*) leading to a spelling confusion.

   (e) *I go*
  – Overgeneralization that the future can always be referred to using *will*.
  – Ignorance of the rule governing time clauses with future reference in English.
  – Failure to appreciate that *will* is not a tense but a modal indicating either willingness or a present decision about the future.

   (f) *isn't she?*
  – Interference from a mother tongue which has a fixed question-tag form (eg *n'est-ce pas?*).
  – Ignorance of the rules of question-tag formation in English.

   (g) *went*
  – Failure to distinguish between the present perfect = indefinite past and the simple past = definite past.
  – L1 interference (ie interference from a mother tongue which does not make the distinction between definite and indefinite past).
  – Overlearning of present perfect = recent past.

   (h) *lend*
  – L1 interference (ie from a language which has the same lexical item as the equivalent of both *lend* and *borrow*).
  – confusion from learning both items at the same time.

   (i) *has stolen*
  – L1 interference (ie from a language that has the same lexical item as the equivalent of both *steal* and *rob*).

– confusion from learning both items at the same time.

(j) *so that I could book*
  – Confusion with *so* + V = result.

(k) *went*
  – Failure to distinguish between the past perfect = first of two or more past actions and the simple past = specific action in the past.
  – Overlearning of the past perfect (especially by student whose L1 does not have an equivalent of the English past perfect).

(l) *injured*
  – Overgeneralization of the reference of *wounded*.
  – L1 interference (ie from a language which has one lexical item as the equivalent of both *wound* and *injure*).

(m) *he had asked*
  – Ignorance of the tense sequence of the Third Conditional.
  – Interference from strong association between the simple past and events in the past.

(n) *a friend came*
  – Interference from L1.

(o) *too*
  – Failure to perceive the different roles of *too* and *to*.
  – Pronouncing *to* as *too* (even when the vowel of *to* should be weakened as a result of lack of stress) and thereby adding to the confusion between the two words.

(p) *We couldn't care less*
  – L1 interference.
  – Confusion as a result of learning many English idioms.

(q) *to swim/for a swim*
  – L1 interference.
  – Overgeneralization of *for* + V-ing = purpose of instrument (eg *It's for cutting wood*).

(r) *My mother is*
  – L1 interference from a mother tongue which uses personal pronouns to repeat subjects.

(s) *she*
  – L1 interference from a mother tongue which does not differentiate between male and female in its system of personal pronouns.

(t) *playing*
  – Overgeneralization of S + V + V infinitive.

2 (a) L1 interference.
  (b) False analogy.
  (c) Overgeneralization.
  (d) Overlearning.
  (e) Ignorance.
  (f) Incomplete learning.
  (g) Interference from other items in English.

Commentary

B 1, 2

Error	Correction
I will be football player	I am going to be a footballer
when I will be back	when I go back (or return)
to my home	home
I will be professor	I am going to be a teacher
in school	in a school
What for?	Why?
will enjoy	will enjoy it
be teach	be a teacher
is bore	is boring
will be interest	is more interesting
It will be rich	It will make me rich
Professor will be rich	A teacher is well paid too
not true	that's not true
Football player	A footballer
will be very much rich	is much richer, much better paid
Football player	A footballer
not be rich	is not rich, is not well paid
not give	is not given much money
he will be give	he is given
lot of money	a lot of money

3 (a) ✗ *be football player*

  – no system of articles in L1 (first language).

  – false analogy of football player with tennis player etc.

  – literal translation of football player from L1 equivalent.

  (b) ✗ *be professor*

  – no system of articles in L2.

  – L1 interference.

  (c) ✗ *will enjoy*

  – confusion between transitive and intransitive verbs.

  – L1 interference from intransitive equivalent of transitive *enjoy*.

4 (a) and (b) The learners have made many errors because they have attempted a *free* conversation at an elementary stage of learning and have therefore inevitably made errors caused by ignorance, L1 interference, false analogy and over-generalization. However the two learners have basically managed to communicate and it would be a mistake for the teacher to draw attention to all their errors. This would negate the important feeling of successful communication, would discourage and probably inhibit the learners and would impose far too great a load of re-learning for it to be of any remedial value. It would, equally, be discouraging to the learners to interrupt the flow of their conversation to correct them. Any correction may be better done *after* the conversation on the basis of notes made by the teacher. It would be much more useful to focus attention on errors which the two learners both frequently make (eg the omission of the indefinite article) and on errors which could cause misunderstanding (eg *professor* for *teacher*, *not give* for *is not given*). However if the two learners were having a real conversation (ie not solicited by the teacher) it would probably be a mistake to correct them at all.

C 1 In the first extract the learner has got the past simple tense of the three irregular verbs right but has omitted necessary articles and the pronoun object of *read*. In the second extract he/she has used articles and a pronoun object correctly but has got the past simple tense of the three irregular verbs wrong.

2 In the two weeks he/she has obviously learned how to use the indefinite article and the pronoun as object. However it also seems that he/she has *strongly* learned the regular form of the simple past tense (ie V + *-ed*) and that over-generalization of this form has caused him/her to get wrong what was got right before.

D The learner can use the correct form of the third person of the simple present tense (*lives, cycles, goes, plays, comes*) but gets it wrong after a conjunction (after *but* and *and*). This suggests that he/she has problems with co-ordination rather than with the present simple tense. The learner also uses connectors (*however* and *nevertheless*) as though they were link words. That is, he/she uses them to join two clauses within a sentence rather than to join two sentences together.

E 1

Error	*Correction*
to my bed	to bed
there came a friend	a friend came
died	had died
to meet	meeting
when there were stairs	when we came to some stairs
upstairs	up them
his shin	whose skin
a scarp	a scar
in his face	on his face
beckoned me to come over	beckoned to me
in my back	behind me
holding a gun	holding guns
I went near	I moved near to the man
the man had	He had
died	had died
from an accident	in an accident
I said I could manage it, so he got a lot of money	I said I could arrange it so that he got a lot of money
He would gave	He would give
to do everything in order	to arrange everything
tied on a chair	tied to a chair
We made up a story	We devised a plan
back, they	back. They
He took	The man took
took his knife to my heart	pointed his knife at my heart
want to come near with his knife	tried to attack me with his knife
asked what there was happened	asked what had happened
happened I said	happened. I said

2 *Types of error*
Tense errors
Failure to use past perfect when required
Prepositional errors
Use of wrong prepositions (especially after verbs)
Adverbial errors
Problems expressing the concept of relative position
Word order
Subject placed after verb
Punctuation
Comma instead of full stop
Comma when not required
Spelling
Lexical errors
Most of the errors are in this category
Underuse of connectors
Most of the sentences start with personal pronouns and therefore the logical link between sentences is not always clear.

Possible cause of errors
L1 interference
Direct translation (eg *there came a friend to me*)
Interference from L1 construction (eg *would gave me three hours to do everything in order*)
Overlearning
Simple past always used to make past reference
Interference from similar English expression
eg *shin* (*skin*); *scarp* (*scar*); *could manage it, so he got a lot of money* (*managed it, so he got a lot of money*)
Ignorance
eg complete inability to manage reported speech of past perfect passive (✗ *she asked me what there was happened*)
Using the known for the unknown
eg *story* for *plan*

F	*Error*	*Correction*
	in a little local village	In a little village
	switched on television	switched on his/the television
	had been broken down	was broken
	to get a ladder	so he could use it
	to fix it	to fix the aerial
	so he had to shout	so he shouted
	on earth again	back to the ground
	at home	in the house
	switched on television	switched on the television

G	1	*Error*	*Correction*
		has been taken	had been taken
		but	and
		in hospital	in the hospital

must	had to
after closing time	after visiting time was over
has lonely	was alone
granted him permission	allowed
shortly	for a short time
If he told me he was going	If he had told me he was going
I could give him a lift	I could have given him a lift
would have	could have

2 (a) *lonely* for *alone* or *closing time* for *after visiting time was over*
  (b) *granted him permission*
  (c) *shortly* for *a short time*
  (d) *in hospital* for *in the hospital*
  (e) *He has been taken*

H This open-ended exercise may be used by the trainer to check the ideas developed by trainees through working on the unit.

Conclusion

If you have worked your way through most or all of the material in this book, you have probably found your own view of language developing and changing. We hope you have re-examined some of your beliefs and become aware of new and interesting views of language. Whether your involvement in language comes from the perspective of a learner or from that of a teacher (or from both!), you will probably wish to continue your explorations beyond the level of this introductory workbook. In doing this you will probably wish to examine more and more authentic samples of written and spoken English, and to compare the insights you gain from this with the data you find in grammar books and coursebooks. You will find this rewarding and revealing, and in time you will develop your own, robust, enquiring view of language in all its richness and diversity. Language is an open system, divergent rather than convergent in nature, and once you begin to tolerate the ambiguities and inconsistencies which can exasperate the more dogmatic types of learner, you will find that your own teaching and/or learning will benefit enormously. Good luck – there's no turning back now!

Index

References in **bold** type indicate that the topic is given thorough treatment, or that the whole exercise or section is devoted to it. References to the commentary are <u>underlined</u>. Grammatical terms and notions are printed in ordinary type. Individual words dealt with from a grammatical point of view are printed in *italics*.